OVERCOME
THE OVERWHELM

THE *6-STEP B.R.E.A.T.H.* PROCESS
TO ACCESS INNER PEACE

SAM KABERT

#1 Bestselling Author of SOUL/Life Balance

DISCLAIMER: This book relates to the author's self-experimentation with ayahuasca and is intended to convey the author's experiences only. They are not intended to encourage anyone to break the law, and no attempt should be made to use these substances for any purpose except in a legally sanctioned jurisdiction or as part of a recognized clinical trial. The author and the publisher expressly disclaim any liability, loss, or risk, personal or otherwise, that is incurred as a consequence, directly or indirectly, of the contents of this book.

DEDICATION

This book is dedicated to my parents, Mom & Dad. Thank you for both your ongoing support and belief in me. The past year has undoubtedly been the most challenging time of my life and without you by my side I don't know how I could have gotten through it. From the bottom of my heart, I thank you with every ounce of my being. I love you both and our four golden retrievers (Cali, Riley, Zoobi, and Hana).

My parents have supported and encouraged me throughout my life yet it was within this past year that our relationship got tested more than ever before. With new challenges as a family and my complete loss of belief in myself, it was their ongoing belief in me and seeing me for how I wish I could see myself, that allowed me to finally step into my confidence on a new and greater level. I love you, Mom and Dad.

PRAISE FOR OVERCOME THE OVERWHELM

❝ Sam Kabert nails it in his new book, *Overcome the Overwhelm*. With a keen eye fixed on the dilemma of modern man he expertly guides us back to the root cure all of us need, an expanded relationship with our breath.

— Eben Britton, former NFL athlete turned yogi

❝ Sam Kabert does a great job of consistently reminding us that processing thoughts and feelings is a whole body experience. So much popular mindset advice disregards the inherent intelligence of the body to help us heal and evolve into the person we want to be. Sam, on the other hand, starts with the body and provides the inner roadmap necessary to promote real transformation in our everyday lives.

— Tim Grimes, mindset coach and author of "The Joy of Not Thinking"

❝ At the beginning of my career, I was trying to prove myself with the position I held and how much I could produce in a day. This of course led to years of suffering and eventual burnout that made me question everything. If only I knew the answer to all of my overwhelming feelings was on the other side of my breath, I would have prioritized Sam's 6-Step B.R.E.A.T.H. method a long time ago. It is simple, practical, and can be used at any time of day when you find yourself in a stressed-out state. Plus it is backed by tons of evidence-based research that now proves we can regulate our nervous system using his go-to process. If you are a busy working professional, I highly recommend this book to gain control of your life and achieve the balance your soul has been longing for!"

— Alicia Kay, licensed trauma counselor, LMHC, CLC

" Learning the 6-Step B.R.E.A.T.H. Process and 90 Second Rule have been transformational. By integrating these practices into my daily life my relationships, self-esteem, overall health and well-being have been measurably improved. These simple yet incredibly effective practices have changed the way I process and respond to the emotional ups and downs of life, giving me peace in the most unlikely circumstances. Thank you, Sam.

— Jill Schindler, corporate executive turned spiritual seeker

" *Overcome the Overwhelm* is just what you need during these busy, busy times. The pace of change is not slowing down and if anything, it's speeding up. So many people are trying to do more with less and they're having less and less energy left over to LIVE! Kabert shares a simple six step process to remind us how to BREATHE and live our lives without being overwhelmed. So, take a deep breath, pick up this book, and read. It's a gift to yourself you'll be grateful for.

— Bill G. Williams, author, speaker, and executive coach

" In a world where the relentless pursuit of Work/Life Balance often leads us astray, Sam Kabert's *'Overcome the Overwhelm'* serves as a lighthouse, guiding us towards the transformative 6-Step B.R.E.A.T.H. Process that will help navigate the corporate storms of anxiety and stress, but also learning the invaluable lesson of embracing and transforming emotions, rather than avoiding them. Imagine a world where we allow ourselves the space to feel, process, and accept our emotions—this book is a crucial step towards that paradigm shift, offering a path to inner peace and mental well-being that is both profound and essential."

— Amy Williams, CEO, AB Unlimited Worldwide

" The meticulous B.R.E.A.T.H. Process Sam lays out is essential to allow yourself to be a present, empathetic, and heart-led leader at the workplace and at home. It's allowed me to be at my best by empowering me to tap into and regulate my inner landscape. As a result, my work and the relationships I hold my most dear are thriving due to the tools and knowledge Sam drops in this game-changing book.

— Tony Ferrara, former college athlete turned corporate executive & seeker

" We all feel overwhelmed from time to time. It's how we choose to deal with these feelings that can make the difference. Overcoming overwhelm involves effectively managing the stress that comes from the multitude of tasks, responsibilities, and emotions we face - whether at work, or in our personal lives. In his latest book, Sam Kabert walks us through an easy to follow 6-step B.R.E.A.T.H. process that will transform the way you approach stress and have you on a path to inner peace.

— Laurie Moore, director of operations, PromoCorner

CONTENTS

FOREWORD

PARTICIPATING IN ELITE gymnastics training starting at age three and competing in collegiate athletics provided me with the life training I needed to develop a fine-tuned kinesthetic awareness, indestructible determination, and innate ability to push through just about any obstacle.

In college, I studied a major and minor in both biology and exercise sciences, worked two jobs to keep gas in my moped, and trained a minimum of four hours a day in the gym.

During this time, I was trained to believe being 10 minutes EARLY was LATE. I grew up in my early teenage years and early 20s under the learned axiom you don't put in 50% and get 50% back. Life is all-or-nothing. You always give 100% or more or you get nothing in return.

While this tough outer and inner shell and unfaltering work ethic is what in part drove me to several All-Americans at the collegiate gymnastics level, to obtaining a Doctorate in Physical Therapy, and so many other mountainous feats, these attributes also wound me spiraling down a light-speed slope into a pit of mental and physical fatigue.

We've all felt overwhelmed. I talk to many colleagues within the healthcare field and...well, need I say more than...we are burned out.

When I synchronistically met Sam in Santa Cruz, CA, we shared a similar understanding and found a soul connection in more ways than one.

One of which was our shared experience of understanding what it feels like to show up each day with an unfaltering desire to pursue your dreams, to then go on to LIVE those dreams and yet simultaneously experience a feeling of external and internal BURNOUT.

In this book, Sam provides simple strategies to avoid this life burnout. Now, as a doctor of physical therapy, I see in my patients firsthand the effects mental distress can have on the body.

I find that many common physical symptoms are in part manifestations of our internal state. In the same way that when you feel embarrassed your cheeks get red and when you are about to give a speech you might sweat, your neck might tense, and your heart rate may increase, constant overwhelm can also have physiological effects that show up in the physical body and that impair overall wellbeing, especially when the "overwhelm" is chronic. The manifestations of overwhelm in the body are sneaky and insidious in origin, often occurring within the subconscious mind first, undetected until you suddenly look up to find you too have spiraled to the bottom of the burnout pit.

No amount of muscular strengthening or complex surgery can fix the back pain that comes from chronic tension in the mind because the truth is life will always beg for MORE of you.

Using the strategies in Sam's book as patient education material has served as another valuable tool that I utilize in assisting my patients back to whole body wellbeing. With these techniques, I watch my patients clear their minds and in turn heal the body.

For me these days, I find this to be true.

When we actively seek out space, whether it's creating space internally within the body or externally between the constant "to-dos" on our lists, we begin to uncover *bliss*.

In moments of stillness, we find gratitude growing in our hearts for all the gifts we miss while rushing around.

Without space:

We roll quickly past the sunrises.

Our physical bodies begin to feel overworked, overtrained, and unable to function in homeostasis.

Chronic injuries creep in.

We blow by the stranger who wanted to tell us that our energy shines brighter than the sun.

We miss our parents or children growing old.

*Physically taking space means opening areas of compression within your muscles, joints, and fascia.

*Mentally, this means finding space between the constant chatter in your mind.

Past the radio static of busyness, what exists?

This is the vertigo of silence.

Emerging out of the death of soaring out of control through life on autopilot.

When we choose SPACE, we glide into azure skies, able to experience life rather than watch life pass by... into a world where we find spaces between all of the "must-dos" and "physical tension."

This is life in the *NOW*.

We become consumed with what it means to be alive.

Thank you Sam for sharing this bliss with me and to all who share in overcoming overwhelm.

— Shan Escarra, former college athlete & doctor of physical therapy

CHAPTER 1

Life's Chaotic Symphony

BEFORE EVEN ROLLING out of bed, the pressures of the day already surface. No sooner than the alarm goes off, we're balancing playing with pets and the kids while feeding all the hungry mouths. The endless flood of emails stream in overnight, text messages pile up, meetings ahead, schedules to balance ... time for ourselves is nowhere to be found. As soon as we wake up our needs already turn to others. We are being demanded to respond to situations at hand that require our energy and yet, we remain disconnected from the most important thing of all: *how we feel on the inside*. So, what do we do? Well, we wake up and turn on the pot of coffee in an attempt to best prepare ourselves for the obligations ahead.

As you sip your warm and comforting morning concoction, in enters that suffocating feeling like you can't breathe, doing everything you can to hold it together but in truth drowning deep inside with endless thoughts on loop. As you try to get it together there's little to no gas left in the tank and all motivation to make a change is running on fumes. Lost in desperation, you give in and give up; and ignore how you feel deep within all to just make it through another monotonous day.

These words may hit close to home. You may find yourself nodding your head and resonating all too well, wishing you didn't. What's happening now is your body is sending you a signal to associate these words you're reading with past experiences. This is a trigger – triggers aren't necessarily good or bad, it all depends on the narrative that *you give* that trigger.

In the process of experiencing a trigger, your mind may shift to fear and/or panic. This is how simple it is for us to switch into fight or flight. Now I don't know anyone that would openly desire this state of panic and fear. It is my aim to help guide you through identifying these deeper feelings so that you can move past them and overcome overwhelm.

This book is for the overworked or nearly burnt-out professional – the workplace leaders who want to drastically shift the way they do business and prioritize *themselves*. But before we can even get into changing the workplace to prioritize psychological safety and our overall mental health, we must first do some inner work.

In *Overcome the Overwhelm* you'll learn the 6 steps to ... well, get past the chaotic state of a mind circling with thoughts that bring about feelings of anxiety, stress ... and, you guessed it ... overwhelm.

I'm giving you the exact blueprint I've used to transform my own life. In the past few years, I've shared these steps with other overworked professionals & ambitious leaders through teaching yoga, leading breathwork journeys, speaking on stages to corporate audiences, and working with private clients in group programs and one-on-one settings.

Let's begin by taking a deep breath in together ...

Go ahead; with me now, inhale through your nose and as you inhale feel the expansion of your belly as you breathe into the very top and you can't inhale anymore. Then ever so slowly begin to sigh the breath out of your mouth.

Do it again. Through the nose inhale, all the way up, and gently exhale through the mouth. One last one and on this one let out some noise as you exhale.

Okay, one more for good measure. Let out any remaining breath before inhaling, and when you're ready to inhale imagine you've been deep under sea observing the beautiful colors, fishes, sea urchins and all the magnificent beauty of a reef in the tropics ... and you're just coming up for air now and getting settled on the boat. You look around and feel gratitude for the experience you're currently having, and you close your eyes and through your nose, you inhale as deeply as you can, taking a slight pause at the top of your breath, and ever so slowly you begin to release the air out from your chest down to your belly and you let your shoulders relax and you sink into the present moment.

Do you notice any subtle shifts in how you feel?

Connecting to your breath is one of the most and paradoxically profoundly simple things you can do to overcome overwhelming feelings.

Unfortunately, overwhelming feelings of panic, anxiety, and fear are all too common in our society. The pulse of the professional landscape beats with the urgency of a ticking time bomb as our stress continues to compound with never-ending demands. We race through our day, dodge distractions, and try to beat the clock to meet our urgent demands all while maintaining some sort of balance to keep potential fires at bay.

In a moment of clarity, just a moment, because that's all time allows; we find ourselves asking ... *"Is this .. really, my life?"*

And as soon as this question comes through, another demand of your attention comes in so you shove that thought down and respond to lend a helping hand.

It's nearly impossible to "turn off" and "unplug" from not just work responsibilities, but life responsibilities. Having a pocket-sized laptop on us at all times sure does make life convenient, yet it also keeps us distracted from just simply noticing our thoughts and how we feel. The overwhelming chaotic state of our existence is ever present and it will continue to build if we don't find ways to slow down, unplug, rest, breathe, and just simply be without doing and trying to achieve something.

There is a way to rise above the chaos, cut through the noise, and find inner peace. In this book, I'm giving you the 6 secrets to transform your life from overwhelm to inner peace. It begins with being honest with yourself and exploring the parts of yourself that have been potentially getting neglected for years.

The Shadow Self...

Exploring our Shadow Self

Take Control of Your Life by Making the Subconscious Conscious

Hi, my name is Sam and I'm thrilled to go on this journey with you. Now, before we begin, I would like to warn you that this book is about going deep, it's about what well-respected late psychiatrist Carl Jung would call "Shadow Work".

❝ One does not become enlightened by imagining figures of light, but by making the darkness conscious
- Carl Jung

Shadow work is a big term and to simplify it, we can view this philosophy as exploring the subconscious parts of one's personality. Make no mistake about it, shadow work is not easy nor is it often pleasant. When you apply the teachings from this book, you'll be getting uncomfortable. If it feels easy, you can most likely challenge yourself to go deeper.

Shadow Work is like a Russian doll, you just keep revealing layers of your Self. Each new layer may potentially bring new challenges and suppressed thoughts, feelings, and memories to the surface. The moment you say that the discomfort from the layers of "the work" being peeled back are enough and you give up, is also when you're no longer doing shadow work ... but if you're willing to go deeper and reveal those layers and truly see and feel them ... Well, that's Shadow Work. By feeling these emotions we're able to transform them and that is the purpose of shadow work. It is by descending into the depths of the psyche to reveal and let go of the unprocessed emotions that catapults us into the higher vibrations of love, joy, and peace.

The "shadow" represents aspects of one's psyche that are often denied, repressed, and hidden. On a subconscious level (what you don't have conscious awareness of), many of us wear metaphorical masks to hide these undesirable aspects of our psyche (or personality). Now, I know I said I was going to simplify "shadow work" and I just threw out a few big terms, so, for the sake of getting on the same page, let's now define these terms.

Conscious Mind: Dictionary.com defines conscious as being "aware of one's own existence, feelings, thoughts, surroundings, etc." It's been said that the conscious mind makes up just 5% of our total awareness.

Subconscious Mind: Meriam-Webster dictionary defines the subconscious as "existing in the mind but not immediately available to consciousness". The best way to understand the subconscious mind, as explained to me by one of my teachers, is through this simple exercise. Right now, go ahead and wiggle your right big toe. You just brought your subconscious awareness of your big toe to conscious awareness. You could feel your big toe all along, but until you were prompted to wiggle it, you didn't have conscious awareness of it. Our subconscious mind makes up just 95% of our total awareness which means that we are only consciously aware of 5% of our thoughts and feelings.

Psyche: Meriam-Webster defines psyche as "soul, personality, the totality of elements forming the mind".

Our conscious awareness is literally how we move through life with intention. It's when you sit down and ask yourself "What is it I really want in life?" Think about how you would run a meeting or set goals for yourself, this is consciously choosing how you move through life.

Whereas our subconscious awareness can, at times, keep us stuck. For example, in the past few years, as I've dove deeper into my own psyche, I've discovered a subconscious pattern of self-sabotage. Now, I'd never intentionally sabotage myself, that just doesn't make sense, does it? However, I kept having these patterns where I'd put myself into undesirable situations - how could this be? Well, it was my subconscious guiding me to those areas and this is why it's so crucial to bring our subconscious mind to light, so we can bring more intentionality to our choices and decisions through conscious awareness.

Carl Jung famously said, "until you make the (subconscious) conscious, it will rule your life and you will call it Fate". In this book, you will learn how to take back control of your life through making your subconscious conscious.

The formula of Shadow Work is as follows:

Awareness: First, making the declaration to accept and recognize the existence of the shadow aspects within oneself.

Exploration: Secondly, utilize various mindful practices to help identify specific parts of the shadow. In this book, you'll learn some of the more practical exercises to explore your shadow.

Acceptance: Without judgment and shame, true acceptance will be necessary to transform the subconscious thoughts and feelings that are keeping you in a state of overwhelm.

Integration: Finally, it's time to incorporate the insights gained from this deep process and make the necessary changes in your life. The process of integration (taking action), and making changes in your life is crucial to overcome overwhelm.

I like to think about shadow work as feeling our emotions. Many of us will do anything we can to not feel and will turn the other way toward a distraction to numb ourselves. I'm speaking from experience. I had years of abusing alcohol, using work as a way to avoid my deeper existential angst, and my addiction to fantasy football as a way to keep me busy and keep in touch with my friends. This book isn't about my story, although I will be sharing some of my journey with you to illustrate how I've overcome my own overwhelm in recent years. If you want to go deeper into my story, I wrote an entire other book about my spiritual awakening journey called *SOUL/Life Balance: A Guide to Igniting & Integrating Spiritual Awakenings*.

Overcome the Overwhelm isn't about me, it's not about your partner, your family, your closest friends, your colleagues, or your clients ... It's about YOU!

It's about getting uncomfortably familiar with all the isolated parts of your psyche. It's about diving into your subconscious awareness so that you can move beyond the beliefs that keep you stuck. It's about stepping into your worth, boldly claiming who you are, and living a life in alignment with your true self.

The process I'll be sharing with you is known as the 6-Step B.R.E.A.T.H. Process and yes, 6 steps can be tricky to remember so what I really want you to remember are these 3 simple themes:

Theme #1: BREATHE

The very first step in overcoming overwhelm is to slow down and to connect with your breath. When you feel a heavier emotion, notice that and allow yourself the time to breathe into it. Deep inhales and longer and slower exhales. I'll be walking you through this step and the remaining five steps later in the book; for now I'd just like to give you a taste of what's to come.

The second step is centered around allowing yourself to feel what's arising in you. Emotions are energy in motion, so allow yourself to relax into the energy knowing it will move through your body in 90 seconds if you accept it rather than deny it.

Theme #2: FEEL

The second theme is about getting curious about what your feelings are here to teach you. All of the energies within (from stress to grief to anger and so on...) are here to guide us in different and unique ways. As such, step 3 is about allowing the energy within to reveal something to you. But what exactly is stress? Stress is simply our body's response to pressure. According to the Mental Health Foundation, many situations can cause stress, but it is often triggered when we experience something new or unexpected that threatens our sense of self or when we feel we have little control over a situation. The good news is that we have more control over our stress than we may think.

> **❝** Stress is not what happens to us. It's our response to what happens and the response is something we can choose **- Maureen Killoran**

From this point on, we'll learn how to guide ourselves from stress and into a calmer state on command.

The hardest part in all of these steps (for most people anyway) is when we first begin to look for the lesson within these denser energies. Many of us don't want to accept what may come to the surface. Yet it's only when we see the lesson of what's being revealed that we are able to move through the heavier feels. It's for this reason that step 4 is all about acceptance.

Theme #3: THINK INTENTIONALLY

The third theme of the 6 steps is about transforming subconscious feelings into conscious and intentional thinking. Positive affirmations alone don't work because they disregard the deeper underlying issues. In this fifth step, it's time to transform the heavy emotions into an empowering positive "I AM" statement (or belief). We get stuck like a hamster on a wheel when we don't take action and make positive changes. Finally, for step number 6, it's time to reflect on the previous 5 steps and find a new habit and/or action to take to evoke positive change in your life.

I hope you can feel my excitement as you read these words. Make no mistake this will be a journey of highs and lows. This is shadow work. We will be leaning into some uncomfortable edges and for good reason as we anchor into the purpose of doing this work to overcome overwhelming feelings as opposed to just pushing them down like so many of us have spent a lifetime doing. In return, we'll overcome overwhelm and guide ourselves into more enjoyable states of being in a few simple steps.

CHAPTER 2

72 Ounces to Freedom

I HAVE ALWAYS loved reggae and Sublime's "40oz. to Freedom" – it was a go-to album for me back in my high school days. Yet, for me, it was 72 ounces and a large pizza that led to my freedom.

Sometime in the fall of 2017, I did what all great entrepreneurs do when faced with adversity so intense it could be the end of your business as you know it ...

I ordered a large pizza and got myself a 6 pack of my favorite hazy IPA.

Earlier that year my first podcast with my buddy Sergio Oliveri called "WhatUp! Silicon Valley" started to take off. I hired my second employee and began outsourcing everything that didn't require my skill set. I had finally found my freedom, only to watch it slip away just as quickly.

It wasn't working out with my second employee, so, unfortunately, I had to let them go. Not long after that, my right hand for the previous few years had turned in their resignation. I went from freedom to being sucked right back into mundane tasks.

That faithful night, you know the night of 72 ounces to freedom, well ... that was the night I decided to make a change. I decided I wouldn't go back to being a slave to my business. I wouldn't go back to being burnt out and overwhelmed. I wouldn't go to sleep until I found a solution and find a solution I did. After many phone calls with friends in business that I trusted most and sitting with some deep questions; I made the intentional decision to radically shift my business from an employee-based business model to a freelancer-based business model. This worked for me because I had a small boutique promotional products marketing agency. I could operate on a lean business model. At the time, I had read Tim Ferriss' well-respected "4 Hour Work Week" some years earlier and had always dreamt of cracking the code on how to scale my business with virtual assistants (freelancers).

Now, don't get me wrong, it took even more time to fix the cracked foundation in my business and rebuild it with a new team. But in time, I restructured my business model and became so well-known for my skillset in scaling my own business with virtual assistants that I became known as "The VA Guy". In 2020, I was named to the promotional products industry's list of "Rising Stars". The promotional products industry is made up of over 150,000 people, it's a 25 billion dollar industry and each year they name 12 people to their list of "Rising Stars". I don't say this to brag. I say this because I know you're a hard worker at heart as well. I'm here to give you a glimpse into my life at the time so that you can feel in your nervous system the drive one must have to reach this level of success and overcome overwhelm. I say all of this to flatten your learning curve – because the pursuit of my goals nearly cost my life. Forget about burnout and overwhelm, I was dealing with existential angst.

When Our Core Wounds Come to the Surface

Ever since I can remember, I've always had a chip on my shoulder and the thing is, I don't have many memories before junior high. It takes a lot of time to sit in reflection, journaling, and other healing modalities for me (and many others) to access early memories. Recently, I was reflecting on my relationship with quitting because I noticed some recurring patterns in myself related to quitting. Upon noticing these patterns, I was thrown off, because I'm no quitter. I built a million-dollar company, was named to Silicon Valley's 40 under 40 list, and have written 5 books (previous to this one) and the list goes on and on. I am not a quitter.

Yet, I am starting and quitting quite a few things as of late. Before we get into the root of this core wound here, let's take a brief moment to look at identifying yourself with labels. If I were to identify as someone who doesn't quit, I would overlook this recurring pattern of quitting and dismiss it because I resonate with being an overachiever as that is the label I identify with more than anything else. This way of logical thinking is basically saying, "Hey, I don't quit things, this isn't happening because I'm not a quitter; I'm a builder, I'm a creator, I'm an overachiever" ... fill in the blank, you get the idea. The problem with identifying with a label (specifically in this scenario) is I'd be bypassing the Truth. I'd be avoiding the reality of my actions (or lack thereof) all because of identifying with a label that summarizes who I am and how I show up in the world.

As humans, we're consistently evolving and changing. Nothing stays the same, not even our attitude or our mood. In fact, science teaches us the body has a 90-second physiological response when we experience an emotion.

The theory of constructed emotion explains how emotions happen and are built up. We humans construct our emotions based on two things: our physiological experience of a situation and our personal interpretation of it. This also gives us the power to manage and control our emotions. Dr. Jill Bolte Taylor, Harvard brain scientist explains:

"When a person reacts to something in their environment, there's a 90 second chemical process that happens in the body; after that, any remaining emotional response is just the person choosing to stay in that emotional loop."

Our emotional triggers or red flags activate chemical changes within our body which puts us on full alert: the fight, flight, or freeze response. For these chemicals to be totally flushed out of our body takes less than 90 seconds.

Said another way, when we experience an emotion (which is energy in motion), the body feels this energy and that is what we call emotions. So, take a deep breath in with me now ... go ahead and exhale through your mouth, slowly inhale up through your nose, through your nose again (without exhaling) breathe in a bit more air, and hold the breath for a few seconds, and as slow as you can exhale through your mouth. Allow yourself to feel whatever emotions come up.

When we take time to slow down we can create awareness of how we're actually feeling. It's quite simple and I will expand on this later in the book. For now, I just wanted to get to the point of awareness.

Without finding ways to bring more awareness to our thoughts and feelings, we won't know what's going on within us and in my case (in this example), I wouldn't have recognized my patterns of late in quitting. When I did see these patterns of quitting showing up, I started to journal about it, and as I journaled about it, a memory came through ...

I don't remember my age; let's call it 9 years old. My parents signed me up for tee-ball (or baseball - I don't remember nor do I know which is appropriate for that age and soon you'll learn why) ... It was my first time ever playing the sport and I got sick before the first practice. I ended up missing a few practices and soon after I threw a temper tantrum like a spoiled brat refusing to join the team. This is my earliest memory of quitting. I didn't learn how to swing a bat and throw a baseball til my early 20s. I had avoided any social situation having to do with baseball all because of this underlying core wound of quitting.

Now as I'm older, I can reflect back and piece together other times in my life where I've quit and how that lent to my mentality of overachieving in my career. Almost, in a way, to make up for lost time and to prove to myself I am not a quitter. The underlying issue for this all is not feeling worthy. If you had asked me just a few years ago when I was still avoiding the deep inner work if I felt worthy, I would have smiled and said "YES, of course!" Yet in truth, back then, I had no idea how I felt on the inside. Like so many of us, I was just working away, chasing my dreams, and focused on building a business that could support my lifestyle.

From Breakdown to Breakthrough

When I started my first business (SwagWorx.com) back in 2011, I moved back home to Silicon Valley from Northern California as there would be more opportunity to grow (in business) in Silicon Valley rather than in the rural area of Chico, CA. I didn't want to move to Silicon Valley, I felt like the area lacked a "soul" (if you will). I saw moving to Silicon Valley literally as "doing my time". I would say this often, it was as if I was speaking into existence that I viewed my time in the area as a negative commitment I was bonded to. Yet, I made the most of it, for business purposes.

Remember when I spoke about not only burnout but the deep existential angst I went through as I dove into my business priorities? Here's what that looked like – I'd bet you'll relate.

You see, I lived in Silicon Valley for about 7 years (between 2012 and 2019). During my time there I was on the board of multiple non-profit organizations, chaired a young professionals group, and even created a media network that hosts podcasts and in-person events that partnered with some of the larger organizations in the area. Everything I did in my 7 years in the greater San Jose area was centered around business. My life revolved around business.

I hit burnout several times and I didn't know what to do. I would lay on the couch for hours on end eating unhealthy food drowning in my self-pity. Then when it was time to get to work I'd merely force myself. It was as if I had an on / off switch and I was a soul-less robot. In early 2019, my burnout hit a pivotal point in my life and I couldn't ignore it anymore.

Work/Life Balance is a Myth

I really did have it all. I had achieved what I was chasing. I had built my business into a million-dollar company while working less than 4 hours a day, my girlfriend at the time was a 49ers cheerleader (my favorite team), and I was getting external validation through being named to Silicon Valley's list of the 40 most influential business leaders under 40 years old and was named to my industry's Rising Stars. On paper, I had it all. Yet, something was off...

I knew for quite some time that something was off and rather than looking at it, I numbed it with distractions. That's the thing about overcoming overwhelm – one surefire way to tell that you aren't in touch with how you're truly feeling inside is if you're distracting yourself with what you do each day. For me, fantasy football was my life outside of work (ridiculous, now in hindsight as I look back on it) and my other coping mechanism was food and beer. I didn't want to feel because, to a certain extent, I knew that if I did feel my emotions, I wouldn't like what it brought up and I subconsciously was sabotaging myself to avoid sitting with the deeper questions that would address my existential angst.

In high school, I remember thinking to myself that I wanted to obtain this elusive state of Work/Life Balance. Work/Life Balance was beginning to emerge (at least within my own consciousness at the time) and my interpretation of it was achieving a state where you can flow between enjoying your life without being a slave to your work. This is the very first issue I have with Work/Life Balance; it implies there's an end destination.

Matthew McConaughey said it best in his Oscar Winning Speech, and I'll paraphrase it. He spoke about chasing his hero, and that he would never catch his hero, because his hero was always 10 years ahead of him. This speech resonated with me from the moment I heard it, he's speaking Truth and we can feel that (or at least I can). What McConaughey was alluding to in this speech is that focusing on an end destination is a recipe for disappointment.

To name your Ultimate Potential is to limit your Ultimate Potential.

I saw *my* Ultimate Potential as building a lifestyle business that afforded me the luxury of doing what I wanted when I wanted to do it. I saw building a million-dollar business as my cap. I saw being named to Silicon Valley's 40 under 40 list as the most elusive success I could achieve. I named my Ultimate Potential and in the process, I limited myself.

I had reached my destination. I had hit the summit of the mountain I had been climbing. There was nowhere higher to go, other than going down and go down I did.

I've documented my spiritual journey through my previous book, *SOUL/Life Balance: A Guide to Igniting & Integrating Spiritual Awakenings*, which details my journey of going within and my spiritual awakening – you can find that book on Amazon both in print and audible on the QR code below. For the purposes of this book and staying on topic, for now, I'm going to skip how that process started and what it looked like as it transpired.

My intention with *Overcome the Overwhelm* is to bridge the gap between spirituality (mindfulness) and workplace culture. This book is for the business leaders who are seeking to create a culture of prioritizing Mental Health in the Workplace. This book isn't about my backstory, this book is to give you the tools that I have been using for the past 5 years that have propelled me into a life of purpose, intentionality, fulfillment, joy, and love. Everything you will learn here can be applied to yourself as much as it can be brought into the workplace.

In this book, you'll learn the science behind regulating your nervous system, multiple exercises to invite a more harmonious mental well-being, how to create space for mindfulness in the workplace, and most of all, the process of cultivating awareness.

As you may be able to tell by now, I have a gripe with this notion of Work/Life Balance and it isn't just for the reasons I've listed above. Please just take a second and look at these words that follow ...

Work/Life Balance

Why is the word "Work" before "Life"?

If anything, let's call it "Life/Work" Balance.

I realize the term "Soul" can be triggering for some and for that reason, it's important that when I use the word "Soul", I'm simply referring to one's inner world. Our inner world is made up of our emotional, mental, and physical state. Whereas the outer world is how we experience life through our 5 senses. Similarly, we can look to the wisdom of the Yin Yang.

Yin energy is about our inner world, it's our emotional, mental, and physical state. It's about how we feel more than anything else. Whereas Yang energy is about our outer world, it's about how we show up and move through life.

SOUL/Life Balance is a reframe of Work/Life Balance. We prioritize our own mental health first and foremost through connecting with our inner world while re-categorizing Life to include work.

In *Overcome the Overwhelm*, I'll be sharing with you how to practice SOUL/Life Balance and apply it in your life as just that ... a practice ... so that you can show up in your life (and work) with more energy and enthusiasm!

A quick note on the word "practice" ... I once heard a yoga instructor say "practice makes practice" and it struck me to my core because engrained in my psyche had been "practice makes perfect". The trap of perfection is to get us in a chasing energy with an underlying belief that we aren't enough and that we need to seek out this perfection in order to feel whole. Yet, this isn't true, we aren't chasing perfection.

Now let's revisit what we examined earlier about Work/Life Balance being spoken about as if it's an end destination. For the sake of your own mental well-being, when applying SOUL/Life Balance, I invite you to see it as a practice; meaning that it's a way of life. There is no end destination, there's no chasing involved, it's coming back to yourself through awareness. You will have some days where you feel more connected to your inner world and less connected to the outer world and vice versa. That is okay! That is part of the practice, we are finding balance and grace with where we're at, and through this awareness, we can make shifts in our lifestyle to bring about more ... balance.

CHAPTER 3

What is Overwhelm Anyway?

I RECENTLY ASKED someone how they were feeling and they said "overwhelmed". I sensed they were feeling anxiety and I didn't want to project what I had felt they may be experiencing so I led this person through a series of questions. As we unpacked it more, it came through that yes, they were experiencing anxiety and it was masked as overwhelm.

It's easy to say we feel overwhelmed. Overwhelm is all-encompassing from stress to anxiety, to having a clinically diagnosed burnout, and may even lead to a full-on mental breakdown.

As a leader in the workplace, you're no stranger to stress and burnout. But what's the difference? As mentioned earlier, stress is our *immediate* response to challenges. Our body often presents a surge of energy that propels us into fight or flight. We'll learn how to change from fight or flight to rest & digest later on.

Burnout, on the other hand, is the long-term accumulation of stress that remains trapped within our bodies. You may be experiencing burnout if you feel that you're in a perpetual state of exhaustion, especially at work.

At its core, the overarching term "Overwhelm" indicates it's the first sign of a deeper underlying condition that needs to be addressed. It's much easier to apply a metaphorical band-aid in a subconscious attempt to mask an underlying emotional state that ought to be addressed. We can easily notice when we feel overwhelmed, and just as easily we can choose to distract and numb ourselves with any of our vices; and sometimes we're not even consciously aware of this choice at all.

Over the years some of my vices to numb myself from feeling have been emotional / binge eating, watching sports / movies / shows, abusing alcohol, and most frequently diving into work-related projects to avoid having to feel my feelings. These are just some examples of how we can mask overwhelm and pretend like we're not overwhelmed because we are switching our focus to something that seemingly brings us more joy. Yet, is it really bringing us joy and fulfillment or are we using these things to just avoid an underlying condition?

Overwhelm... the Merriam-Webster dictionary defines this big and often used term as "to overpower in thought or feeling". Now, please stay with me here for a second, as I'm going to get a little deep with you ...

Thoughts & Feelings Create Reality

Spiritual teachers and Science both teach us that our **thoughts and feelings** create our Reality. Earlier I referenced my previous book, *SOUL/Life Balance: A Guide to Igniting & Integrating Spiritual Awakenings*, going deep into the nature of existence and reality, and I want to stay true to this book and avoid going too deep. That said, it is important for us to address how our thoughts and feelings create our reality; as we just learned that

Merriam-Webster defines overwhelm as overpowering thoughts and feelings. Let us connect the dots and make the connection that if we do not have conscious access to our thoughts and feelings, we may be creating more challenges than necessary.

Dr. Joe Dispenza (Dr. Joe), a well-respected voice in the space of merging Science with Spirituality has the following to say about thoughts and feelings creating one's personal reality. First and foremost, Dr. Joe is quite often quoted as saying...

❝Your personality creates your personal reality.

Let that one sink in for a moment ... Additionally, below is a direct quote from Dr. Joe that extends upon how our thoughts and feelings create our personal reality.

❝*The thoughts that you think are the electrical charge in the quantum field. The feelings that you emote are the magnetic charge in the quantum field. The thought sends the signal out and the feelings draws the event back. So, if you're walking around your life, feeling sorry for yourself and feeling like a victim, you are broadcasting that signature into the field and you will create more experiences to suffer.*

For simplicity's sake, let's examine what we just read. First off, we can think of the "quantum field" as the unseen world; this would represent the dimensionality outside of this earthly plane beyond our five senses of three-dimensional reality. We could go deeper no doubt on this, but to keep this basic, let's just think of the quantum field as outside of time and space (how we experience being a human on Earth).

Next, Dr. Joe states that when we feel something, we are sending that feeling outside of time and space (where all creation is born). After thinking about whatever it is we may be thinking about, we are bringing a feeling that correlates with our thoughts back into our physical and emotional bodies.

In essence, negative thoughts and feelings will bring more negativity into one's life, just as positive thoughts and feelings will bring more positivity into one's life. In many ways, these are just science-proven facts that back up why affirmations are so popular and utilized within personal development. Although, **affirmations alone** do not work.

Many of us get stuck in stacking (false) positivity onto unprocessed thoughts and feelings. We say all the things ... you know ... everything about how you want to feel, what you want to achieve, and how you desire to move through your life. Yet, we get stuck and we wonder: *"Why aren't these affirmations working for me, while they are working for so many others?"*

The reason is simpler than you may think ... beneath the veneer of positivity lies dormant unprocessed thoughts and feelings. Said another way, the conscious mind is saying one thing, while the subconscious mind believes another. Please keep in mind that our subconscious mind makes up 95% of our total awareness. It's for this reason why it's crucial to engage with Shadow Work to allow the subconscious to express and release old thoughts and feelings, so that, we may train the subconscious awareness to feel safe enough to embody the new thoughts and feelings through affirmations. If we fail to allow the subconscious to embody our affirmations, they won't actually manifest anything better into our lives.

Identifying Subconscious Limiting Beliefs

2023 was in many ways, the most challenging year in my life, and yet at the same time, I had so much growth! In hindsight, the deep dive I've been doing on my own inner world over the past several years has just been preparing for what was to come in 2023. Had I not been prioritizing my own mental health (and really shadow work) in the years leading up to 2023, I don't know how I would have come out on the other side of the challenges I experienced that year.

What I want to instill in your core belief system is the mentality of asking the question, "How's this happening **for me?**".

Several years back I was introduced to this philosophy of life events and circumstances happening for me, rather than to me, and let me tell you ... this was the paradigm shift I needed to shift my consciousness from a victim mentality to empowerment!

Victim Mentality is when we get lost in thought loops that stem from a core belief of things happening to us. I once heard Dr. Joe Dispenza say that we have 60,000 - 70,000 thoughts a day and 80% of those thoughts are coming from the day before. Well, if that's not wild enough, what's more is that of those 70,000 thoughts a day from the previous day ... 90% of those thoughts are negative! This isn't your fault – in many ways, we're actually programmed to have negative thoughts and beliefs about ourselves and the world around us. Just keep in mind that the reason your life may feel like it's running on autopilot is because your *thoughts* are running on autopilot, habitually, from the day before. It's for this reason that it is imperative to find ways to access our subconscious limiting beliefs because those negative thoughts are what make up 95% of our awareness.

In 2023, when I was faced with the most challenging circumstances in my life, I saw it as an opportunity to dive even deeper into my subconscious and truly feel that all of it was happening for me. I created a process on how to access subconscious limiting beliefs and transform them into empowering limitless beliefs and I will be sharing that process with you throughout this book. Again, what's more important than anything else, is to allow yourself to feel.

Science has a lot to teach us about how to shape our reality through thoughts and feelings. Neuroscience teaches us that our body has a 90-second physiological response whenever we experience an emotion and emotions are energy in motion. So, if we constrict when we feel by distracting and numbing ourselves, we are not allowing that energy (that is in motion) to pass through our nervous system. A big part of why we feel so much overwhelm is that we are carrying a lifetime of unprocessed emotions in our bodies (not to mention traumas). An important additional note is that we all experience trauma in our lives and it's crucial to not compare our trauma. If you think you haven't experienced trauma in your life, think again. That belief is keeping you from feeling, accepting, and allowing those traumas to move through your nervous system.

❝The traumatic event isn't what causes long-lasting trauma, it is the overwhelming trapped response to the perceived life-threat that is causing an imbalanced nervous system. Diffuse the power of the narrative and remap the body memory to regain aliveness and flow. Taking time is very important—as body time is much slower than cognitive time or emotional time **— Dr. Peter Levine, PhD, Creator of Somatic Experiencing**

Gabor Mate, a physician, New York Times Bestselling author, and speaker also known for his work relating to trauma, stress, and early childhood development, says the following about trauma: "trauma is not what happens to you. Trauma is what happens inside you as a result of what happened to you".

When you identify with the trauma you experienced and/or experiencing more trauma than others in your life, be careful ... identifying with your trauma can potentially lead to a victim mentality where this becomes your identity and your personal reality because your personality is made up of being a wounded being. My intention with Overcome the Overwhelm is to provide a safe space and process for you to fully feel unprocessed emotions (stuck energy) and even traumas so that you can clear them out and begin to create the new habits and routines that will lead to more inner peace.

The 2 Types of Overwhelm

To understand the two types of overwhelm, we must first understand what the terms "inner world" and "outer world" mean. As a reminder, our inner world represents our thoughts, feelings, and emotional state. Our outer world is how we experience life through our five senses. The practice of SOUL/Life Balance, at its core, is about bringing intentionality to your inner world throughout the day. Whether it's carving out the space to create (or enhance) a meditation routine, utilizing a daily journaling practice, or if it's as simple as just closing your eyes for a minute a few times a day to just connect with your breath ... to slow down ... to feel ... and to hear and be with your thoughts, without resistance.

#1 External Overwhelm

The first, and more obvious type of overwhelm, is external (or physical) overwhelm which relates to your outer world. It's everything that you may encounter that has to do with your 5 senses. It's the "Life" side of "SOUL/Life Balance".

Examples of External Overwhelm include the following:

- Work Pressures & Stressors
- Personal Obligations
- Financial Responsibilities
- Maintaining a Healthy Lifestyle

The demands of external overwhelm are constant and unavoidable as these represent the foundation of Maslow's Hierarchy of Needs (Physiological Needs, Safety & Security). In my experience, we cannot escape these physical overwhelming obligations. They are ever present and at the forefront of our attention and dictate how many of us move through our lives.

Our responsibilities tend to guide our actions towards others rather than focusing on ourselves first. It's beyond cliche to say these days, yet it is so true, so I'll say it ... We must put on our metaphorical oxygen mask on first before helping others. Literally, any time you fly, you'll hear the preamble which states to put your oxygen mask on first, in the case of emergency, before helping another. I believe that we should live our lives this way as well because if we aren't addressing our own needs first, there's no way we'll be able to show up and support others as our best self.

The overwhelming external pressures of our existence have a way of distracting us from putting on our own metaphorical oxygen mask. Yet, at the same time, when looking at Maslow's Hierarchy of Needs we can see that the foundation of the pyramid is quite literally about taking care of our physical needs first. In order to overcome the physical overwhelm, we must identify our top stressors in physical form.

MASLOW'S HIERARCHY OF NEEDS

Throughout this book, we have provided lines in the book for you to journal and reflect on what you're learning. In the book, "The Artist's Way", the author, Julia Cameron, speaks on the style of journaling known as "Morning Pages". I like to refer to it as Daily Pages as well so it's not limited to just writing in the morning. That said, the style of journaling is writing for 3 pages in what's known as "Stream of Consciousness" writing. Stream of Consciousness writing simply means to not overthink it, just write. The aim of this style of journaling is to not set your pen down until you are done. When you pause, you allow yourself to think. Whereas if you can just continuously write even if phrases like "I don't know why I'm doing this" come through, that's fine! Just keep going. I'll tell you from my own experience and many of my friends, colleagues, and clients that when most of us start this practice we do experience some level of resistance yet when you push through that resistance often something will end up being revealed to you that you didn't know was there previously. SO, as you progress through this book and come across the journaling exercises, I encourage you to not overthink it and just write ... let whatever comes up flow through you. It may just help you identify & get unstuck from something that's been bothering you in your life for years.

Additionally, you may find yourself thinking at some point, "I don't know what to write, it sure would be nice if he offered some examples". The reason why most of these journaling prompts won't offer examples is because that is planting a "subconscious seed" within your psyche. My intention is for you to be as clear as you can so you're not subconsciously thinking about something that I may have planted so that we can get to your Truths, which are, of course, always going to be unique to you.

JOURNALING EXERCISE

#1 External Overwhelm

In the lines below, answer the question, "What are some of my External Overwhelms?" Don't think, just write, let it flow ...

#2 Internal Overwhelm

Internal (or emotional) Overwhelm has everything to do with your Inner World and it can be simply a racing mind and as deep as an underlying lack of purpose and direction in one's life.

Some examples of Internal Overwhelm include the following:

- Past / Future Thought Loops
- Sensitivity to Energy
- Societal Pressures (i.e., Body Image, "Shoulds", "Have to's", "Need to's")
- Existential Angst
- Grief, Sorrow, Worthiness, etc.

The thing about internal overwhelm is it isn't quite as obvious as external overwhelm. Identifying external overwhelm is easy because it's what keeps many of us in a state of consistent fight or flight. External overwhelm is directly correlated to stress as it's the daily obligations and responsibilities that keep one from experiencing inner peace. Whereas with internal (emotional) overwhelm, it's usually harder to identify, because it's beneath the surface. Emotional Overwhelm may represent subconscious thoughts and feelings that are unknowingly guiding us through our lives. Earlier we spoke about Shadow Work and now we'll dive into some shadow work by getting a layer deeper than Physical Overwhelm to identify some of the underlying emotional overwhelms that may be keeping you stuck.

In the lines below, just jot down the first thing that comes to mind, please do not overthink it - just write!

JOURNALING EXERCISE

Do you often think about the past and future? Are your thoughts more geared towards the past or the future? How do you feel when you think about past and/or future thoughts?

Do words like "should", "have to", "need to" swirl in your mind often? If so, why do you feel it's necessary to have these thoughts? Are these thoughts serving? Are these "shoulds", "have to's" and "need to's" based on your own belief systems or do they have to do with societal pressures? What would be helpful to help you let go of these thoughts?

Do you often worry that you're not living up to your fullest potential? Do you think about the meaning of life or have a connection to any religion or spirituality? How do you relate to the notion of having a grandiose purpose for your existence?

Do you experience grief, sorrow, or a lack of worthiness from time to time? When you do experience these (or similar emotions), what do you do when they come up? In your darkest moments, how do you tend to cope with these emotions?

Well done and CONGRATULATIONS! This is just scratching the surface of exploring Shadow Work and it's some of the foundational elements required to overcome overwhelm!

I know it's not easy to answer these questions. I'm proud of you for doing this work and more importantly, I'm encouraging you to find that pride for yourself! Take a moment to close your eyes, connect with some deep inhales and exhales, and send love to yourself. I know this may sound a bit cheesy at first, but seriously ... let go of any limiting thoughts. Just take some deep breaths, maybe even place a palm on your heartbeat to feel your heart, and send yourself gratitude for showing up for you ... not for anyone else ... take this time to practice true self-care and feel what it feels like to be you. Take as much time as you need and if it's feeling especially "heavy", please take some time to get out in nature without your phone and just go on a mindful stroll for a few minutes.

Great work, I'm proud of you!

Remember, at its core, overwhelm is the signal that represents unprocessed emotions and traumas stored within the body, and by doing this work; you will begin to overcome those overwhelming feelings that plague you from living a life of joy, fulfillment, and ultimately inner peace.

CHAPTER 4

Creating the Space & Intention Setting

MY INTENTION AS your guide in the process of overcoming overwhelm is to show up for you with the utmost dedication to guide you along this journey.

Additionally, it's to make these teachings as accessible as possible to lower the barrier to entry to make it easy and accessible for you to integrate what you learn into your daily life. And most of all my intention is to create a safe space to aid your growth and expansion. With that in mind, below is some additional information about creating space and how to bring more awareness to your internal dialogue.

This book is intentionally short so it's easy to consume, take action, and make part of your life. No excuses. When you sign on the dotted line you aren't committing to me or anyone else, you're committing to yourself!

Holding Space

Over the years, I've cultivated my capacity to hold space for others through facilitating hundreds of healing experiences and my extensive training in yoga instruction. Additionally, my experience in leading men's groups and certification as a "Somatic Breathwork" practitioner have contributed to growth in this area.

But what does it mean to hold space, and why does it matter?

I resonate with Steven Jaggers' (founder of Somatic Breathwork) definition of holding space. Here it is ...

> **"** Having developed the ability to take in the full capacity of a moment through neutral consciousness and not being reactively involved but response-able.

What I love about this is that oftentimes when we interact with others, we're simply just waiting for our turn to speak. Take a moment and reflect on one of your more recent deeper conversations...

Can you think back and remember how you may have heard a thought or perhaps even a voice that rose to the surface while the other person was speaking?

Most of us struggle with this and that's okay! What's important is that you bring conscious awareness to this and through practice we can soften these thoughts that arise when others speak.

To truly hold space for another, rather than projecting what's arising within us upon another; it's more important to soften and to fully be present with them to see them and to hear them. And often when those projections come through, that message that makes its way to the surface isn't always for the other person...

often it's for ourselves.

The ego will project upon another to protect itself from going deeper on its own healing journey.

To Hold Space is to Be Present, Period

With all of this in mind, I'd like to take a moment here to shift our gaze inward even more as we aren't talking about holding space for others ... Rather, we're learning to hold space for ourselves ... to prioritize ourselves first and foremost and create the space to soak in and absorb the teachings from this book and commit to yourself to apply and in the process integrate the lessons learned into your lifestyle. According to the American Psychological Association, we tend to downplay our own stress; around two-thirds of adults (67%) reported feeling like their problems are not "bad enough" to be stressed about. But remember that *all* of your emotions are worthy of attending to. To hold space for yourself is to honor your needs and be with the process without resistance.

How Can We Create Space for Ourselves?

Creating the space for your healing to overcome overwhelm is really as simple as bringing intentionality back into your life. Think of it this way ... most of us who journal; just pick up a journal, we sit (or lay) down, and begin to write. When we're done with writing, we put the book down and carry on with our day.

To "create space" is to slow down and bring more intentionally into any specific area of your life.

In the journaling example above, creating space could look like working with palo santo and/or sage, closing the eyes, taking a few deep breaths, allowing an intention to come through, then begin journaling, then when finishing finding gratitude and (maybe even prayer) before moving on with your day.

To me, this is literally the easiest example to create space around one simple practice. Really, it's all about intentionality and slowing down. So much of this work is that simple ... to bring in more awareness - slow down and be more intentional with your energy.

What is Your Intention?

Now it's time to set your intention and before you do so, I'd like to invite you to do the following to create the space to slow down and write an intention you can stick to. Please feel free to modify this process to fit what resonates with you most.

Begin, by finding 5-10 minutes or so where you know you won't be disturbed. You could even go out in nature and take some additional time to be with the elements to find stillness.

- If you'd like, you can begin by working with sage to clear out any negativity and blocks and bring forth positivity into your energetic field with the help of palo santo.
- Close your eyes and take a few moments to conduct a body scan (notice how you feel in your body) with slow and deep breaths focusing on letting your exhales be longer than your inhales.
- Take some time to let any lingering thoughts soften, and come back to your breath as an anchor to let these thoughts pass on by.
- When you're ready, ask yourself a question ... maybe it's as simple as "what is my intention in reading this book?" or maybe "how can I show up for myself best?" or just intuitively

ask a question and pause to wait for the answer to come through.

- When you find your intention, keep your eyes closed (still sitting in meditation) and find some time to sit in gratitude. Gratitude for yourself, for everything you've experienced in your life to get to this moment right now and send some love back to yourself for no reason at all other than to practice what it **feels like** to experience unconditional love for yourself.

My intention is:

I commit to myself (sign & date below)

_____

_____

_____

_____

_____

_____

CHAPTER 5

The Foundations of Breathwork to Overcome the Overwhelm

CONNECTING WITH THE breath is the access point that begins the journey of healing which is what the path of overcoming overwhelm is all about! This path has its curves as it does its bumps, yet when you stay connected to your breath, you'll be able to absorb the ups and downs of the rocky road ahead.

It's worth emphasizing that overcoming overwhelm requires deep healing (shadow work) and understanding how our nervous system works and the breath's role in creating homeostasis within is paramount to your growth in this process.

The nervous system is a term often used, yet not always understood, at its core when you hear the words "nervous system", know that it's the system that includes your brain, spinal cord, and a complex network of nerves. Its role is to broadcast messages back and forth between the brain and the body as it controls our ability to breathe, move, see, think, and feel.

How We Can Calm Our Nervous System

Let's imagine your body is like a town, stay with me as we ignite our inner child's imagination, to understand this intricate system.

The busy town, full of people with things to do and places to be, the town that represents your body that's always on the move. Now, picture your nervous system as a charismatic Mayor orchestrating the dynamic rhythm of the town (your body). The Mayor's role within your body is to make sure everything runs smoothly and the symphony stays in tune. The Mayor (nervous system) has two main functions; first the brain and second the nerves. The brain is the control center while the nerves are messengers that carry important information throughout the town (your body).

Now, when you're making decisions, like how you want to spend your time or what goals you're setting for yourself, your brain sends messages to your body through the nerves. These messages travel instantaneously; as soon as you have the thought, it's sent out through your body. When you feel excitement or even if there's a bit of (perceived) danger, your nervous system kicks in! The nervous system's role is for protection, so it reacts as if the bat signal went off in the town and it morphs into Batman to save the day! This is what is commonly known as "fight or flight" mode (the sympathetic nervous system). Remember your body is the town in this scenario, and if the bat signal is going off, what does that mean? The town is in panic … the body is in panic mode. And what about when the town is saved, what happens then to the town (the body)? The resting state is when the parasympathetic nervous system kicks in which represents "rest and digest". This is relaxation, this is what should be our natural state. Yet, due to the overwhelming nature of life, it has become increasingly challenging to shift into rest and digest. Don't get me wrong, the sympathetic nervous system (fight or flight) has its role and it's vital to our survival, yet at the same time; it ought to be the state we shift into when needed as opposed to our natural state. In fact, it's much easier than you think. Our feelings are already correlated with different breathing patterns. When we feel content, our breathing is slow and regular. When we feel anxious, our breathing is shallow and rapid. When we change how we breathe, we change how we feel.

In summary, the nervous system and our breath are intricately intertwined and consciously changing our breathing patterns holds the potential to shift our nervous system into either fight or flight (sympathetic) or rest and digest (parasympathetic). In the rest of this chapter, we'll explore the growing popularity of breathwork, the science of breathwork, and the breath's vital role in your healing journey. This chapter is the most extensive in the book and contains the most nutrient-dense information as it will serve as the foundation for overcoming the overwhelm ... With that, I invite you to grab a pen, a highlighter, a journal, some tea ... whatever it is you need to take notes and let this information absorb like a sponge.

The Foundations of Breathwork

An online data and research website called Glimpse shared that breathwork grew 40% from January of 2023 to January 2024. In fact, breathwork is increasingly being included in corporate wellness programs as a tool for stress management and promoting a positive work environment.

While breathwork may have gained massive interest in recent years since the lockdowns, it's by no means a new practice. Yoga is said to be around 5,000 years old and one of the eight main foundations (limbs) of yoga is centered around Pranyama which is a Sanskrit word that means "Breath Control". Prana means life energy / breath, while Yama means "control". Oftentimes, Pranayama is referenced as the life force energy that travels through our body by practicing specific breathwork exercises.

When we reflect on the growth of breathwork in recent years, it's quite fascinating because it's actually the one function of the body that we can both control consciously and sub-consciously. We all know how to breathe because we've been doing it our whole lives; yet, as we unpack the science behind breathwork, we'll begin to see that maybe we don't know how to breathe ...

James Nestor published a book entitled *Breathe* in May of 2020 that has taken off like wildfire in our collective psyche as it's sold over 2,000,000 copies (as of January 2024 when I'm writing this book you're reading now). In Nestor's book, he shares his 10 years of researching breathwork that led to his book, Breathe. It's a fantastic book to learn more about the science of breathwork and for our purposes, I'm going to share what I've learned since becoming a certified Breathwork Practitioner as well as a certified Yoga Instructor along with my own personal studies and fascination for this magical force of energy that lies dormant within each of us.

The Science of Breathwork

The data is in and science supports what the yogis of ancient times have known all along, breathwork heals! It doesn't have to be a complicated style of breathing, what's most important is to find breathwork exercises that resonate with you that you'll actually stick with.

Below is a list of some of the top benefits of engaging with a breathwork practice.

- Strengthens immune system & releases toxins (70% of the body's toxins are released through the lungs)
- Reduces stress, anxiety, and depression
- Increases energy, clarity, and peace of mind
- Enhances creativity, innovative thinking, and decision-making
- Develops better communication and a stronger bond among people
- Increases memory, focus, and productivity
- Positively impact sleep quality, leading to better rest and more energy when you wake up
- Reduces unexpected days off
- Decreases burnout

The American Institute of Stress reports that "75% of employees believe that workers have more on-the-job stress than a generation ago". Not only that, but 80% of workers actively experience stress on a daily basis and reported that they desire help in learning how to manage their stress! In fact, stress has become so intense that "25% have felt like screaming or shouting because of job stress".

Breathwork heals workplace stress, period.

We must find ways to improve our own mental well-being to overcome the overwhelm so that we can bridge the gap between mental health and workplace culture. Connecting to one's breath is single-handedly the most accessible and efficient way to improve one's own mental, emotional, and even physical well-being.

Vagus Nerve

The vagus nerve, also referred to as the vagal nerves, are the primary nerves that make up the parasympathetic nervous system (rest and digest). The National Library of Medicine confirmed just a few years ago that one session of deep and slow breathing reduces anxiety. The science-backed hard fact is that the vagus nerve becomes activated through certain breathing exercises and it's the vagus nerve's role to help guide the body into rest and digest. When the vagus nerve is activated, it triggers a relaxation response as opposed to "fight or flight". In the process, the heart decreases, blood pressure stabilizes and muscle tension decreases.

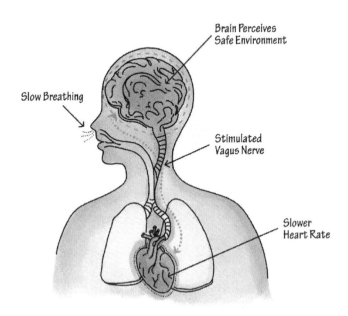

The vagus nerve, also referred to as the vagal nerves, are the primary nerves that make up the parasympathetic nervous system (rest and digest). The National Library of Medicine confirmed just a few years ago that one session of deep and slow breathing reduces anxiety. The science-backed hard fact is that the vagus nerve becomes activated through certain breathing exercises and it's the vagus nerve's role to help guide the body into rest and digest. When the vagus nerve is activated, it triggers a relaxation response as opposed to "fight or flight". In the process, the heart decreases, blood pressure stabilizes and muscle tension decreases.

Cortisol

Cortisol, the stress hormone, is extremely prevalent in the chaotic environment that contributes to overwhelm, and by practicing breathwork you're actually reducing cortisol levels. When the vagus nerve is activated it influences the release of cortisol which leads to less anxiety and overall stress.

Heart Rate Variability (HRV)

The intervals between heartbeats is what is known as HRV and a higher HRV is associated with improved stress resilience and emotional regulation. Another benefit of activating the vagus nerve through breathwork is that in doing so you are improving your heart rate variability.

Healthy Gut

Our guts are actually known as a second brain and Harvard researchers have encouraged professionals in the greater field of psychology to "consider what's happening in the patient's gut" as an approach to improved cognitive health. With that said, the vagus nerve plays a role in regulating digestion as well which we now know is linked to improved mental health.

The research to support breathwork as a gateway to overcoming the overwhelm is vast and it will continue to grow with the massive and fast-growing interest in breathwork. I don't know about you, but I'm so encouraged by the interest in healthy habits like breathwork because it's no secret humanity as a whole needs ways to reconnect with their inner world more than ever before.

CHAPTER 6

The 6-Step B.R.E.A.T.H. Process

BEFORE WE GET into the 6 steps to overcome overwhelm, I'd like to invite you to approach the rest of this book as you would if you saved up thousands of dollars dedicated solely to your own healing. Imagine you have planned for a trip to a foreign country and your passport is all you need to get to your destination.

That same level of preparation and excitement is the mindset I'm encouraging you to adopt as you prime your psyche for the steps ahead. I'm hoping you can learn from my past endeavors of various trainings and retreats to accelerate your own healing.

What I'm teaching you in this book has the potential to transform your life, period. For that to happen though, you'll need to be invested. I've done many training sessions from yoga trainings to breathwork trainings along with other healing retreats and many of them have contributed to my own healing and ability to teach others.

Yet, a common theme I've noticed in the process, is when I commit to these deeper dives, I am telling myself that I need to show up for myself because I'm invested. Yet, when I sign-up for an online course, read a self-help book or am doing something similar on my own; I tend to not be as dedicated.

This isn't always the case, for example, I've studied Dr. Joe Dispenza's book, *Breaking the Habit of Being Yourself*, and have taken meticulous notes so that I could really apply his teachings into my life. The point I want to drill home to you is that just because this is a book (a low cost investment), it doesn't mean that it doesn't have the potential to massively change your life!

Additionally often we look at either a training, a retreat or anything similar as an opportunity to learn from others and have them facilitate healing for ourselves. In essence, what we do is we're outsourcing our healing and bypassing our own sovereignty as we subconsciously tell ourselves to ignore our own inner compass that knows what's best for us. However, in truth, healing happens when you take back the reins to apply what you learn and integrate into your life.

If it's helpful, rip out the previous pages where you wrote out your intention and committed to yourself with your signature and date of when you made this declaration. Then tape it to your bathroom mirror, put it in your wallet, leave on your desk, or anywhere else that seems appropriate.

My role as a teacher is not only to provide education but to inspire you to take action! To integrate means to take action. Think about the last conference you attended, you likely were motivated, maybe even inspired to take action. When you came home, what happened?

For many ... nothing.

If you don't take action after inspiration strikes, you will not see results, period. The taking action piece of learning is the integration of what you now know being applied into your life and this is where change and transformation occur.

With that, let's begin and emerge our psyches into the 6-Step B.R.E.A.T.H. Process to overcome overwhelm and shift into a more harmonious state of being!

integration of what you now know being applied into your life and this is where change and transformation occur.

With that, let's begin and emerge our psyches into the 6-Step B.R.E.A.T.H. Process to overcome overwhelm and shift into a more harmonious state of being!

CHAPTER 7

Step #1 - BREATHE to Slow Down

THE FIRST STEP in the B.R.E.A.T.H. Process is to slow down. Let's face it, the world moves fast, (especially for ambitious hard workers like us) so fast in fact, we often-times forget to breathe. Our breath is actually the only bodily function operating without needing our conscious awareness.

However, oftentimes we hold our breath. We hold our breath in all sorts of situations ranging from when we are vigorously typing out an email, when we're reading (like you are now) and the issue with holding your breath is it activates the fight or flight response which is not necessary in these examples.

While you're reading this, typing out an email, or anything similar, start to notice how you hold your breath. In doing so you're contributing to a state of fight or flight as opposed to being more consciously aware and intentional with deep long and even longer and slower exhales you can shift into rest and digest.

The overwhelming feelings we experience are so intense that we often tell ourselves "I don't have time for mindfulness." In reality, mindfulness doesn't need to take a chunk of time out of your day; at its core, mindfulness is simply about awareness of the present moment. Meaning that what you're about to learn in this book will not be about adding more to your to-do list, this is a direct path to cultivating moment to moment awareness.

The truth is you always have a choice and you'll need to choose to be more intentional with your time. You don't need 20 minutes a day. All you need is to bring this to the forefront of your awareness and start to make small shifts and changes that help you overcome overwhelm.

The steps within this book are utilizing the acronym "B.R.E.A.T.H." for a specific purpose and that is simply because connecting with your breath, understanding its role in the nervous system and how it affects our physical, emotional and mental state is crucial to overcoming overwhelm. So with that in mind, let's begin by simplifying the term "breathwork".

Simplifying the Term "Breathwork"

Breathwork is a big term that is getting tossed around without a clear definition of what one is talking about when they use the term. This is a struggle within the breathwork community and something that I'm extremely passionate about teaching and encouraging people to understand if they desire to learn more about breathwork. For simplicity's sake, I'm going to break down breathwork within two buckets. The first being breathwork for release and the second being breathwork for rest & digest.

#1 Breathwork Journeys (For Release)

We'll begin with breathwork journeys centered around activating the sympathetic nervous system to release stored energies within our body. As we've learned earlier in this book, emotions are energy in motion and science teaches us that our bodies have a 90 second physiological response when we experience an emotion. So, with this in mind, if we constrict by numbing and distracting ourselves from feeling said emotion, that energy will get stored within the body. Moreover, we all experience trauma and it's important to remember not to compare our trauma. Trauma is trauma, period. In fact, trauma can be anything that overwhelms your system in the moment. So, not only is the body holding onto unprocessed emotions from daily stressors and as far back as childhood, but we're also potentially carrying onto unprocessed trauma as well.

The aim of a Breathwork Journey is to mimic a trauma response by activating the sympathetic nervous system which puts us into a fight or flight mode to allow the body to release these stored and unprocessed energies within the body. Imagine you're in the Serengeti and you see a lion. This lion is stalking a herd of gazelle, and as it slowly approaches them, the lion finds one to attack. The lion thrusts its body on this gazelle and does its best to take it down to bring it back to the pride so that they can nourish themselves. But, the gazelle gets away ... as the gazelle gets away, it starts to shake and convulse ...

What's happening here is that the gazelle just experienced a traumatic event. Literally, it was scared for its life as this lion was about to kill and eat it, so what did the gazelle do? It naturally took the time to feel the trauma and shake it out of its system. Within minutes you'd see this gazelle chomping away on the foliage from Mother Earth's offering to keep the gazelle alive. As humans, more often than not, we do the opposite, we constrict, we do anything to avoid having to feel negative energies and as such these energies get stuck and stored within the body. Whereas in the animal kingdom the 90 second rule of feeling the energy to allow it to be in motion occurs naturally.

In fact, Somatic Experiencing (SE™) is a clinical methodology created by Dr. Peter Levine based upon this acknowledgement that animals in the wild are not traumatized by routine threats to their lives, while humans, on the other hand, are readily overwhelmed and often subject to long-lasting traumatic symptoms of hyperarousal, shutdown, and dysregulation. It's all because they allow it to pass through their systems.

I was trained in "Somatic Breathwork" which is a 60 minute practice to focus on creating a safe place for people to express these unprocessed energies so that they can release them. I like to say that it's called "breathwork" because it's work! The first half of these breathwork journeys are intense as the aim is to get the ego self (conscious mind) out of the way so that the body can do its thing and release all of these energies that are keeping us blocked in our life. Whereas the second half of the experience is about restoration and rejuvenation so that we can call in how it is we want to feel in our body and move beyond the session to integrate the newfound peace into daily life.

These breathwork journeys utilize a circular connected breathing technique coupled with rhythmic music to produce a cathartic emotional release. This release may be in the form of moving, shaking, yelling, crying, or laughing. Through this intense breathing technique, we are able to engage in the innate ability to heal and sweep out any defenses, blockages, restrictions, or pains that hold us back from how we want to show up in the world. A breathwork journey, to me, is the ultimate experience of feeling what it is to be a spiritual being embodied in human form. After my first experience with a breathwork journey, I had literally felt reborn, and this isn't uncommon.

Rebirth Through a Breathwork Journey

February and March of 2019 was the rock bottom I needed to shake me up to awaken my spirit. I was numb. Sleepless nights. Lost. I didn't know what to do, I was literally drowning in a sea of sameness: of monotony, without purpose, unable to access gratitude, and stuck. Enter a breathwork journey.

A friend had told me about how she did a breathwork journey and at the time I was all ears and open to anything because I was so desperately seeking something to transform my negativity into anything remotely positive at all. At the time I had just gotten into a normal yoga routine as yoga finally clicked for me a year previously when an instructor cued our breathing during the postures in a way that connected me to the power of breath unlike before. I have been practicing yoga off and on since college (2008 ~) yet, mostly I was off as at the time I was very concerned about my image and my more "meathead" type friends would make fun of me for doing yoga (silly, now in reflection, I know).

So, it wasn't until 2018 or so that I really got into yoga and became committed to the practice. And when my friend told me about her experience with a breathwork journey, I was fascinated; more than anything else because I was just beginning to scratch the surface on how connecting to our breath intentionally has the power to change our entire emotional, mental and physiological state.

I still remember my first breathwork journey back in early 2019 when about halfway through I noticed my body vibrating. Not shaking, but vibrating. And it was almost like I could see myself lying on the mat and hearing the words from my facilitator yet I wasn't in my body. It was like my Soul left and it came back to hear my facilitator cueing me to breathe slower and deeper and in so doing I surrendered. I let it all go, I came back into my body feeling eternal bliss and peace. I paint this picture because I want you to fully understand that while a breathwork journey is safe (there are some contraindications), it is imperative to know that this is a deeply spiritual experience.

Many conferences are now offering breathwork journeys which I think is fantastic! Yet, at the same time, it's really important to know what you're offering and getting yourself into. I'm hopeful and enthusiastic to see the corporate world offering breathwork journeys as a way to drastically shift the mental health of their employees, clients and vendors.

In early 2023, I was invited to be part of a breathwork journey for a team of 100 or so salespeople. Most of the people in the room were men and were stereotypical salespeople (not to feed into stereotypes, but just keepin' it real ... think ... mid 20's / early 30's "jock" type). By the end of the session, nearly every single pair of eyes was doused in tears. It's a beautiful thing to see a group of people (especially co-workers) come together to release their stored energies within their nervous system.

#2 Daily Breathwork Exercises (Rest & Digest)

While I like to think of the aforementioned "breathwork journeys" as maintenance and not a daily practice, breathwork exercises to activate the parasympathetic nervous system are something that I would recommend building into your daily routine. I've tried a lot of various breathwork exercises and I'll share a few of them with you, however, there are many resources whether it be on YouTube or an in-person class/workshop to experience these breathwork exercises to help you learn which styles will resonate most with you.

Overwhelm can strike at any point in time, which is why I want to emphasize the importance of learning these breathwork exercises to shift into rest and digest as opposed to encouraging you to lean into breathwork journeys. The breathwork journeys can be thought of as cracking you open to release the stored energies keeping one stuck, while the breathwork exercises that activate the parasympathetic nervous system are to help integrate your new desired state of being into daily life. I typically recommend breathwork journeys once annually, once a quarter, once a month and only weekly or more frequently if you're currently facing major challenges. The daily practice of simple breathwork exercises that activate the parasympathetic nervous system is crucial to include as part of your lifestyle to overcome overwhelm.

James Nestor, the author of *Breathe*, teaches that many of us are what we would call mouth breathers. Meaning that we have our mouth open when we're not speaking because we're inhaling and exhaling through our mouths as opposed to our nose. If you are a "mouth breather", I encourage you to research Nestor's work and recommendations to tape your mouth when you go to sleep to teach your body to breathe through your nose. Please do your own research and find a route that is safe and works best for you. The challenge with being a mouth breather is that breathing in and out of the mouth, per Dr. Andrew Huberman, activates the sympathetic nervous system (fight or flight). Whereas inhaling and exhaling through the nose activates the parasympathetic nervous system (rest and digest). So, a simple first practice is to bring more intentionality to your breathing patterns and focus on inhaling and exhaling through the nose – the best part is you can do this anytime, anywhere.

Another big tip to overcome overwhelm while utilizing your breath to self-regulate your nervous system is to focus on elongating your exhales. It's been proven by Dr. Huberman's lab at Stanford among other researchers that allowing your exhales to be longer than your inhales can help shift your nervous system into rest and digest. A simple exercise here could be to close your eyes, notice the sensitivities of how you feel and what you hear to find a little stillness within, you may even roll your neck out a bit to help free your spine so you can sit straight up, then slowly inhale through your nose, and when you exhale just let your exhale be longer than your inhale. Nothing fancy, just resting, slowing down, connecting to your breath with slow inhales and even longer and slower exhales.

A fascinating tidbit is that when you exhale, it's not as important that you exhale through the nose, exhaling through your mouth with an audible sigh (making a noise) can be very effective in calming your nervous system down. Try this exercise for a few minutes and just notice how you feel. You can come back to this simple practice of elongating your exhales at any point in your day. When you're in a meeting, when you're reading, when you're stressed ... literally any time. And as you practice this, your body will naturally start to do it on its own more so that you are now training yourself to breathe in a more calming sort of fashion allowing for deeper inhales and exhales as opposed to the shallow breathing that many of us do.

Speaking of shallow breathing, try noticing your breath when you read or write. I find that when I'm writing sometimes I'll be holding my breath. Although in recent years as I've made such a conscious effort to notice and transform my connection to my breath, it's much more rare that I find myself holding my breath. When you do notice that either your breaths are shallow or you're holding your breath, no worries, just notice that and thank yourself for noticing and come back to long and slow deep inhales and exhales.

I also practice elongating my inhales and exhales when I'm conversing with others, whether it be in an informal catch up with a loved one or a professional business meeting. Connecting to my breath while talking with other people helps me to relax, have less thoughts about what I'm going to say next and ultimately be more present with the conversation and other person I'm connecting with.

Scientifically speaking, the practice of the Cyclic Sigh has been shown to be more powerful than any other breathwork or meditation practice it was compared to, to alleviate stress and anxiety per a study by Stanford Medicine and Dr. Andrew Huberman's team of researchers. In the next chapter, I'll walk you through the basics of the cyclic sigh and provide a QR code to practice this exercise along with me guiding you through every step of the way. For now, let's just focus on slow inhales and exhales in and out of the nose to keep it super simple.

Breathwork Basics: The "3 Rules"

There are 3 basic "rules" of breathwork I'd like to teach you that will be your north star to overcome the overwhelm.

Rule #1: Elongate those exhales ... I mean it, really focus on letting your exhales be longer than your inhales. It's these extended exhales that contribute to shifting your nervous system into rest and digest.

Rule #2: If you notice that you keep your mouth open when you're not speaking, you're likely a mouth breather. If you're a mouth breather, then please check out James Nestor's teachings on safe ways to train your body to begin to breathe through the nose. Breathing through your mouth is more likely to activate fight or flight. Even notice as you're reading these words right now ... are you holding your breath? Are you breathing shallowly? Or are you connected with your breath? I encourage you as you continue to read these words to focus on inhaling slowly and deeply through your nose and allow your exhales (through the nose) to be longer than your inhales. It's this simple process that can help to alleviate stress and anxiety. Remember, as a basic rule of thumb, breathing through your nose will help to contribute to a more restful state.

Rule #3: Lastly, the diaphragmatic breath ... go ahead and inhale ... notice if your belly comes in or out. Let's try again ... inhale through your nose, did your belly come in toward your spine or did it push out? We want our bellies to expand as if we were to blow up a balloon. That is the simplest way to explain a diaphragmatic breath. The Cleveland Clinic reports diaphragmatic breathing contributes to "reducing blood pressure, heart rate, and relaxation".

If your belly does come in when you breathe, no worries, just realize it makes sense that it would and you can just bring more intentionality to letting the belly expand. I actually had to train myself to let my belly expand on my inhales and I totally get why it was difficult. First, when you inhale, you're sucking air in, so naturally, you may want to suck in your belly as well. Secondly, growing up as a bit chubbier kid in my youth and getting made fun of had led me to suck in my gut - so why on Earth would I want to expand (and expose) my belly? There are so many societal norms that lead to poor mental health and this is but just one small example of how wanting to fit in affected my breathing pattern which affected my ability to shift into rest and digest. Bottom line, be proud, let it out and expand that diaphragm on those inhales.

Exercise: Conscious Breathing

In the next 24 hours, notice your breath when ... you're in conversation with someone, when eating, when scrolling through your phone, just notice. Are you breathing through your mouth or your nose? Are you holding your breath? Are your breaths shallow? Does your belly expand when you inhale?

Come back to these pages, leave an earmark, bookmark, or a pen on this page and journal about your experience in the lines provided below.

JOURNALING EXERCISE

In the lines below, write about what you experienced in the past 24 hours as you began to notice your breath.

Integrate & Take Action

Each step will have a corresponding video on YouTube to walk you through an exercise relating to the step. For the first step of connecting to your breath to slow down, we'll focus on diaphragmatic breathing and just getting comfortable with this form of slow breathing.

Scan the QR code below to check out the video and after you practice the breathwork exercise in the video, I invite you to come back to these pages and journal about your experience.

JOURNALING EXERCISE

How did it feel to slow down? What came up for you? What was the experience like? Don't overthink it, just write ...

CHAPTER 8

Step #2 - RELAX to Feel

OVERWHELM CAN STRIKE at any time and sometimes without a warning and even for no specific reason. Remember that overwhelm is that all encompassing feeling representing something deeper; whether it be stress, anxiety or even stemming from old traumas being activated by triggers. What we must keep at the forefront of our awareness as it relates to overcoming overwhelm is that this is a healing journey and to heal we must allow ourselves to feel.

By the way, Healthline, defines a trigger as "anything - including memories, experiences, or events - that sparks an intense emotional reaction, regardless of your current mood".

Through activating relaxation we can begin to feel what's arising to the surface. These feelings are the emotions that have been stored within the body and as you'll recall the emotions are energy in motion. Rather than avoiding these emotions, I'm inviting you to sit with these emotions and allow these energies to move through your body.

Our second step in the B.R.E.A.T.H. process is to **relax** so we can allow ourselves space to **feel** and process overwhelming energies that are ready to move on. Neville Goddard, a prominent mid-20th century spiritual teacher and author, said this about relaxation:

> **"** Relaxation is the opposite of struggle. We don't 'try' to relax; we surrender to peaceful feelings of relaxation. It's a giving in, a letting go, of concerted effort.

Although this is much easier said than done, how would one actually relax if they are feeling tense and overwhelmed? I'll speak for myself at least, because I know that when I'm experiencing a massive wave of overwhelm that is really just cloaked and disguised as overwhelm yet truly it's a wave of anxiety; the last thing I feel able to do is to relax. Yet herein lies the paradox ... it's through the softening and allowance of this anxiety (or whatever emotion it is you're feeling) that it will begin to dissipate. When you tense up, you're constricting and you're contributing to the energies getting stuck. Whereas with relaxation, you're softening and you're allowing the energies to move through you. So, how is it done?

It's actually easier to relax in these tense moments than it seems. We just need to be taught the tools to recognize when these feelings arise and what to do next. You might have already guessed it ... the key to relaxation so that you can feel is through your breath. Specifically, it's by utilizing your breath as a tool to regulate your nervous system and shift from fight or flight to rest and digest.

RELAXATION ... say it with me here ... RELAXATION.

Let's say it again and this time inhale as you say it and say it out loud ... RELAXATION.

Did you feel it?

This word itself carries a soothing energy and it's calming for the mind and the body. Not only does the sound of the word elicit these feelings but the association with the connection of what the word represents sends the body into a deeper sense of ease.

This entire process is known as somatic therapy and it's about allowing the body to experience the stored stress within so that it can release these energies. Now, remember that science teaches us that we have a 90 second physiological response when we experience an emotion. I'll repeat myself over and over again so this drills into your conscious awareness ... emotions are energy in motion and with this in mind, can we soften to allow ourselves the 90 seconds for the body to process these energies so that they can be in motion and not stuck within the body?

Simply, pause, breathe, relax and feel.

Yet again, it's not always so simple, and for that reason we're going to go even deeper on how to shift from fight or flight into rest and digest.

Before we move on, I'll leave you with one additional Neville Goddard quote, "How successful you are on the outside is directly related to how relaxed you feel inside". Remember, Neville also teaches us that to relax, we don't try to relax, we surrender to peaceful feelings of relaxation... it's a giving in."

Identifying & Naming Your Emotions

While this book is primarily about overcoming overwhelm and linked to the lives of "busy professionals" like yourself who experience stress and anxiety on a daily basis, it's also about getting real with all of our emotions and allowing ourselves to feel. VeryWellMind.com, an online resource for mental health awareness and resources, speaks about the 6 types of basic emotions.

The 6 basic emotions, as described by Paul Eckman in the 1970s, are happiness, sadness, disgust, fear, surprise and anger. As we continue with this step (and the process in general), I would encourage you to identify and name your emotions. You can keep it simple with one of the 6 basic emotions as outlined above or name it anything else. The important part of this step is to feel, so allow yourself to feel the emotion that's coming to the surface through naming it. Identifying these emotions is the first step toward guiding yourself into a more positive state of being. Keep in mind that emotions aren't black & white – they are often more gradient, and it's totally possible to feel a mix of happiness, anger, and excitement all at once. It's all about getting in touch with how you feel, accepting it, and guiding yourself into a state of rest & digest.

How to Move into Rest & Digest

Let's bring our imagination to a faraway land with a King and his Queen, princesses and princes, dragons, bridges, knights in shining armor, and a wizard. The castle sits atop a hill overlooking land as far as you can see. Paint in your mind's eye the setting sun in that scene from the movie "Lion King", where Mufasa tells his young cub Simba, "Everything the light touches ... is our kingdom. But, a King's time as ruler rises and falls like the sun. One day, the sun will set on my time here, and will rise with you as the new King". Shifting your gaze from the beauty of the turning of the page from the golds and yellows that make up the captivating setting of the sun, you see the castle behind you.

This castle is your body, and the nervous system represents the knights on guard, ready for protection against any threats that dare come to challenge this kingdom. When danger does present itself, these knights will be ready. Let us not forget the Wizard and his magical ways having the ability to offer an extra layer of protection. The Wizard's secret to bringing order to the land is his teachings of Breathwork. The Wizard teaches that we have the ability to tap into our own innate magic and we can do so through the power of our breath.

By simply intentionally connecting with our breath through slow and deep inhales and exhales, we can activate our own innate and divine right to bring order to our own inner kingdom (or queendom).

In this second step of overcoming overwhelm, I am going to teach you the most important elements to understanding how utilizing your breath can (and will) help you to regulate your nervous system and shift into rest and digest on a more ongoing basis.

Breathwork is like a wizard's spell that helps bring order and peace to the castle. When you take slow and deep breaths, it's like casting a magical calming spell. Your breath sends a message to the nervous system, telling it to relax and take a break and it's in this process that you are allowing yourself to feel those stuck energies that are ready to be released.

The Cyclic Sigh: Ultimate Exercise to Alleviate Stress & Anxiety

Dr. Andrew Huberman's lab, at the Stanford School of Medicine, conducted a study to discover the most effective exercise to alleviate stress and anxiety and their findings concluded that the cyclic sigh is the best practice one can do to overcome overwhelm. The best part of what I'm about to share with you is that it is the easiest and most simple form of breathwork I've ever tried!

Earlier we learned what a breathwork journey is and what it entails. You likely were thinking, "Wow that sounds intense" and it certainly is a massive experience that requires a lot of effort and courage to feel deep emotions and potentially a spiritual rebirth. You may have tried other forms of breathwork in meditation and/or yoga classes similar to alternate nostril breathing, box breathing or a three part yogic breath ... all of these are fantastic, yet they aren't the most user-friendly if you're just starting out.

What I love about the cyclic sigh is its simplicity and how practical it is for anyone to start doing right away and integrate into their daily life! You deserve to start feeling less overwhelmed in the workplace, and your daily life in general, right away.

But before we get started with the cyclic sigh, I'd like to share some context as to why it works. Stanford's study compared various forms of breathwork alongside meditation practices with the aim of learning which would be best to "chronically reduce stress around the clock, improve mood and improve sleep". Literally their goal was to find the shortest and most effective technique to reduce stress not only while performing the exercise, but also "around the clock ... 24 hours a day".

Dr. Huberman shared in his podcast called "Huberman Lab" that the physiological sigh was discovered in the 1930s. During this time, we learned that when people under breathe they have a build-up of carbon dioxide as a result people would do this "psychological sigh" subconsciously. The body is intelligent and the reason the body performs this physiological sigh is to eliminate excessive carbon dioxide and rebalance the oxygen to carbon dioxide ratio in the proper ways. You'll start to notice that when you hold your breath subconsciously, you'll do this physiological sigh.

The physiological sigh happens when you inhale all the way up, then inhale a bit more and release a good amount of air and as mentioned this is a natural occurrence. However, when we intentionally practice the physiological sigh repeatedly, say for about 5 minutes, that is when this exercise is called cyclic sighing. It's as simple as inhaling all the way up, inhaling a bit more, and releasing all of the air.

Dr. Huberman states the following in his podcast about the effectiveness of the cyclic sigh, it is the "fastest physiological way (that we are aware of) to reduce your levels of stress and to reintroduce calm. That is to shift your autonomic nervous system from a state of heightened autonomic arousal" to rest and digest. It's for this reason that I teach the cyclic sigh as a way to overcome overwhelm and quickly shift into relaxation.

In Stanford's study, they asked people to practice the cyclic sigh for 5 minutes once a day. "The people who did that cyclic sighing for 5 minutes a day, regardless of the time of day that they did it, experienced the greatest reduction of stress (not just during the practice, but around the 24 hour cycle)".

Are you ready to practice the cyclic sigh?!

Exercise: Practicing The Cyclic Sigh

#1: Through your nose, inhale as deeply as you can.

#2: At the top of the inhale, through your nose, inhale as much more breath as you can.

#3: Slowly, through the mouth exhale the breath.

NOTE: When you inhale, let your belly expand like a balloon and when you exhale let your shoulders drop and bring your belly to your spine.

I'd recommend setting a timer for 5 minutes and continue to breathe this way and slowly just notice how you feel before going on to the next thing.

In the lines below, just take some time to reflect on how you feel after practicing the cyclic sigh for 5 minutes.

_____

_____

_____

_____

_____

_____

_____

_____

_____

_____

_____

_____

_____

Integrate & Take Action

Now, I'm a practical guy, and for that reason, I'd like to encourage you to hold yourself accountable. It's not enough to just read how to do the cyclic sigh, experiment with the cyclic sigh once, and then go on about your life. Real change comes in the integration, that is in the taking action upon what it is you're learning. It's been said that true wisdom comes from "applied knowledge". So, what are you going to do next?

If you'd like a suggestion, my invitation for you is to put "Cyclic Sigh" on your calendar for 15 minutes for today and the next 2 days. I typically teach to create new habits and routines in the form of a 5 Day Challenge - these 5 day challenges work and it's a great way to build a new routine while also for this one beginning to retrain your nervous system to breathe in a more soothing way that is working for you with around the clock benefits. So, you choose if 2 days or 5 days feels more accessible to you, just be honest with yourself and if 2 days seem more realistic then start with 2 and build from there!

This exercise is for just 5 minutes, I'm suggesting allot 15 minutes for each session so that you have time before and after to just gently enter into your breathwork exercise and not feel rushed to do this as if you're just checking something off your list. Your intentions, as we learned earlier, are extremely important, so please, when you sit down to do this breathwork exercise, allow yourself the space to really drop in and not be distracted as in doing so you'll get even more out of this practice.

Whatever and however you choose to apply what you're learning is totally up to you and what's most important is that you're applying what you're learning and experimenting with what resonates and what does not. The aim, to be clear, of Step #2 is to feel your emotions, it's to slow down and recognize when you're feeling something and to notice when you're subconsciously self-sabotaging with numbing and distractions. It will take time and with dedication it will get easier; remember, just breathe ...

Keep in mind, the entire purpose of this second step is to utilize our breath as an access point to our emotions and to anchor us in allowing ourselves to feel, process and release stored energy in the body.

Below you'll find a QR code that will take you to a video I recorded specifically to walk you through the cyclic sigh. I would encourage you to practice the cyclic sigh on your own throughout your day as needed, yet, at the same time it can be nice to have a guided experience. So, if you'd like to have a guided session to get you going, be sure to scan the QR code below to breathe with me as we take the second step in overcoming overwhelm through accessing the incredible power of shifting our emotional and mental state simply through our breath.

CHAPTER 9

Step #3 - ENERGY to Reveal

WHILE RELAXATION ALLOWS us to feel the deeper emotions, it's in this newfound awareness that we can begin to see the **energies** arising that are **revealing** the greater lessons within us that are asking for tender love and grace. The third step of the B.R.E.A.T.H. process is to use the energy that you're feeling to reveal what aspects of yourself, stories, and past traumas are contributing to the pressure of the overwhelm that keeps you stuck in fight or flight.

Now, let's start with this concept of "stories" because this word alone can easily be misunderstood. I like to think of stories, in this context, representing when we hold onto old patterns and beliefs based on previous life experiences. In other words, I've had a story my entire life that I experienced the condition known as S.A.D. which stands for Seasonal Affective Disorder. For as long as I could remember my depression would lead me into a bottomless pit in the winter months. As soon as Halloween approached it marked the changing of the weather and I had a story that Halloween would be a checkpoint of which we would have shorter days and colder weather and thus my sadness would meet me once again like an unwanted old friend. All of this is true by the way ... Halloween is around the time when the clocks change, the weather gets colder and we're nearing winter. On top of that, I have plenty of past life experience to base my assumption that I'll get sad during this time of year. While this can be true, it can also be extremely limiting, and here's how...

I'm not being mindful of my energy. I'm allowing this **story** to dictate how I will move through this time of year as I'm telling my subconscious mind, which makes up 95% of my total awareness, that the days are shorter and the weather is colder and that means this is the trigger that will activate my sadness. As I've practiced the B.R.E.A.T.H. process for myself, this third step of being mindful of my energy, which includes my thoughts and feelings, has revealed to me how I have a story of allowing the weather to dictate my mood. Furthermore, around the time I started seeing life in this way, I moved from Silicon Valley to the beach town of Santa Cruz. One thing people may not know about beach towns, especially Santa Cruz, is that our summers can feel like Fall or even Winter. And by that, I simply mean that it's often the case from around June to August (give or take) that we won't see the sun til after 1pm or even 2pm.

Science teaches us that our circadian rhythm is regulated by light exposure, and intentionally viewing morning sunlight prepares the body and mind for the day ahead and it's for this reason that many people these days prioritize getting outdoors and letting the sun hit their skin as early in the day as they can.

Now going back to my story, I moved to Santa Cruz in July of 2019 and at the time I was used to 90-degree weather or warmer during the summer months. It was a challenge for my mental health to not see the sun often until the afternoon. However, what this led to was a deeper awareness of the story that had played on loop in my head over the years about the weather dictating my mood. When I allowed this energy of mine to be revealed I was able to accept where I was at so I could move on through the B.R.E.A.T.H. process and ultimately transform that energy to build a new relationship with the weather. I'm happy to share with you now that while I still struggle with the Fall/Winter months, it's not nearly a struggle as it has been my entire life.

I utilize new habits like prioritizing more sunlight and hot / cold therapy (daily sauna and cold plunge) amongst other ways of being that I know will support my mental well-being during this challenging time for many of us. This example in itself is the entire B.R.E.A.T.H. process applied. Starting with being on the healing journey and connecting with my **breath, relaxing** into the process to feel what's coming to the surface, noticing my **energy** to reveal what's asking to be brought to my attention, **accepting** the situation (story of the weather in this case), which in turn allows me to **transform** the story and finally integrating new **habits** so that the transformation will stay at the forefront of my intentions.

It's imperative that on this third step, you really begin to become mindful of your thoughts and feelings as this is the energy that you are sending to your subconscious mind. Carl Jung famously said, "until you make the unconscious (subconscious) conscious, it will rule your life and you will call it Fate". Connecting to our breath and allowing ourselves to slow down and relax into our inner landscape is just the beginning, it's the foundation upon which this process is built and now it's time for us to explore the nature of energy.

Energetic Hygiene

I imagine you take showers, right? I know it's a silly question, of course you shower!

Let's go a layer deeper. Why do you take those showers?

Is it to cleanse yourself?

It's been said that humans are "spiritual beings having a temporary human experience" and as such we are energetic beings. With this knowledge, it's important to not only cleanse our physical body but also our energetic body.

I've intentionally chosen to bring the topic of energetic hygiene into this section because as you go through this process you may become more sensitive to other people's energies. In every single interaction, we are exchanging our energy with other people. If you find yourself feeling drained after certain interactions, it may be because you are literally exchanging energy all the time. Some interactions will leave you feeling more energized, others less energized and some just neutral. What's important is that you begin to notice (or increase) your awareness of how you feel throughout the day. All of this is important because to overcome overwhelm you will need to find ways to bring about more moment-to-moment awareness of how you feel within.

If you do find yourself drained after interacting with certain people, there are some activities you can do to help protect your energy. The main of which is to bring intentionality to your interactions through conscious awareness. As you are interacting with these people, think about putting up an energetic boundary. It's like tapping into your own inner child and going back to when we believed in imaginary friends. Use your imagination to build a force field around you, so that you have protection from what some would refer to as energy vampires. An energy vampire basically means some people subconsciously (and not intentionally) will use your energy to give themselves more energy. You can feel energy vampires, they usually make extremely strong eye contact, are intense with their voice/tone and you're typically left feeling more drained after being around them. No shame towards energy vampires, we all have this aspect within us, even me and even you and it's for this reason it's imperative to get to know our own energy more so that we can take the reins back of our subconscious awareness. If you're reading this and thinking to yourself that you may be an energy vampire, like I said ... no worries. Meditation, breathwork, and this entire process will help to guide you in sourcing your energy from yourself as opposed to draining the lifeforce energy of those around you.

Sometimes, unknowingly, we will get stuck in other people's energy as a way of bypassing our own inner healing. It's as if on a subconscious level, we avoid our own thoughts, feelings, and life circumstances by telling ourselves we are helping someone else with their situation when in reality we are just focusing on their situation to avoid our own. Remember when I spoke about distracting ourselves when it comes to avoiding our own trauma? This is just one of many ways that could play out. This is a dangerous trap that I see all too often, unfortunately. As you find ways to bring about more awareness to your inner state, you will be able to sense when you may be subconsciously helping others to avoid your own thoughts and feelings. If you find that you *do* spend time trying to heal others, consider going back to breathwork and identifying *your* emotions that come up. It's okay to help others, but make note of it and make sure you're making the time to help yourself, too, whether it's getting in touch with your emotions or calming yourself down with the breathwork we touched on.

If you'd like to utilize some tools to protect your energy, you could also grab some palo santo, which is used to add positive energy while sage can be used to remove negativity. It's often said "sage clears out the bad and palo santo brings in the good".

What's important is to realize when your energy is off and come back to a simple practice of cleansing yourself to maintain your own center.

Releasing Energy Within

Earlier we explored breathwork journeys and the intent of said experience to mimic a trauma response so that the body is safe to release stored (and unneeded) energies within. Many people will equate this to when you see a video of a lion chasing a gazelle, if the gazelle escapes, what does it do? It convulses ... it shakes, right? It's literally allowing that trauma the gazelle experienced to move through the body, then in the next scene, you may see that same gazelle grazing on some grass like nothing happened. This is because the gazelle processed what it just experienced and is no longer hanging on to the story of being a victim, having just experienced near death and this traumatic experience yet also at the same time allowing itself to feel and release.

We can also look to little children and see the wisdom of a temper tantrum. While, on the surface, a temper tantrum may be "annoying" and disruptive, it's actually a natural part of the child learning to express itself. The child in this case is using this tantrum as a means to let whatever built-up energy that's unnecessary to the system leave the body. Many of our "core wounds" come from early childhood and it could be as simple as being told you're being too dramatic (or something similar) when you were in your youth; when all you were doing in truth was allowing your process of releasing this stored energy. Unfortunately, when this happens, the prefrontal cortex (the identity part of the brain) is still being developed and now in this situation, this traumatic experience is imparting a new identity onto the child. And this is how core wounds and stories may and do get developed from the early years of our lives.

Breathwork journeys are an intentional practice to go into the depths of the psyche to get the egoic mind out of the way so that the body can do its thing and release stored energies and even traumas. Okay, I just want to back up for a brief moment, because I said another word that has a bit of a mystique around it. Let's unpack the word "ego" or how I used it in the form "egoic" together...

Many of us hear the word "ego" and equate it with narcissistic type behavior yet in the way I'm using the word "ego" or "egoic", I'm actually referring to your identity. Simply put, we can think of the ego as your identity or even your personality. So, when I say to get the ego out of the way when in a breathwork journey, what I'm referring to is the ego (personality) which is what blocks us from releasing stored energy in the body. This is because the energy we hold within plays a major part in building the identity of who we are. To release this energy would be to step into the unknown, and the unknown is uncharted territory which to the ego, on a subconscious level, represents a threat, and therefore the ego can block us from releasing what needs to go. Make sense?

On another note, the ego is not bad, it just is. You may have heard phrases like "the ego is the enemy". This is simply just not true. Thought patterns like that are so black and white and naturally divisive that they just contribute to more internal turmoil. So, now that we're in this rabbit hole we might as well just explore the nature of energy and how you can actually learn from your own energy.

Energy is everywhere. It's in the air we breathe, it's how the weather speaks to us, it's in the cawing of the crows to the squirrels jumping from tree to tree. These energies are alive and are communicating with us constantly. The question is, "Are you aware of it?"

In the B.R.E.A.T.H. process, we're mostly concerned with the energies within your body. As you breathe to slow down and begin to relax so that you can feel what's rising to the surface it's the energy that is revealing something to you. Often it's a lesson and a mindset shift I'd like to instill within you is that everything happens for you, not to you. This is an empowering belief and when you can feel this belief in your core is also when you can begin to allow the lessons to reveal themselves to you.

JOURNALING EXERCISE

What is a story or internal narrative that plays on loop in your mind? Don't overthink it, just write...

Everything is a conscious choice, let's not overcomplicate life, it's within the over-complication that creates a perpetuating loop of overwhelm. Allow what is coming through to come through.

JOURNALING EXERCISE:

Self-Evaluation

What in your life is working for you and what is working against you? Don't overthink it, just write...

It's not only okay to say "NO" but I'd encourage you to say "No" more often! Unfortunately, many of us don't honor our energetic boundaries and needs. Please prioritize yourself first, it is not selfish! You won't be able to show up for others in your highest version of yourself if you don't take care of your own needs first. Remember, what they say at the beginning of a flight, "put your oxygen mask on first before helping others."

JOURNALING EXERCISE

Write about a time that you said "yes", but you really wanted to say "no". Don't overthink it, just write...

Integrate & Take Action

In this exercise, we're going to step up the intensity and get into what I call an activation breathwork exercise. It's a short exercise that will shift you into fight or flight mode to help reveal stuck energies. While breathwork journeys are anywhere from 45-60 minutes (or even longer), this will be about a 5-minute "microdosed" version of the deep cathartic release. It's a lot easier for you to experience this through a video and for that reason, I'm going to spare you from reading how to do it. When you're ready, scan the QR code below and it'll take you to a video walking you through this practice.

I also want to be clear about the B.R.E.A.T.H. process - I am **not** suggesting that you do this exercise daily anytime you feel overwhelmed. You can if you like and if it's something that works for you, however, I'm just simply helping to move things along so that you can feel for yourself the power of the energetic force that lies dormant within you. In normal everyday life, when you experience overwhelm, first I'm inviting you to do some calming breaths to slow down the mind and potentially your heart rate, next relax into it, and feel the emotions that are coming up, and in this step, your focus would be to let those energies reveal something to you. Maybe that something is a story, belief, or old memory … Whatever it is, keep breathing deeply until you access what is being revealed.

Are you ready for some activating breath? Scan the QR code below and I'll see you there!

AND after you've scanned the QR code and joined in on the exercise, you may want to journal about your experience in the lines provided below.

JOURNALING EXERCISE

What came up for you in the exercise? What was revealed? Don't overthink it, just write ...

CHAPTER 10

Step #4 - ACCEPT to Surrender

THE ONLY WAY out is through they say, well if that's true we'll have to find a way to accept this fact and the way to do so is through **accepting** and letting the lesson that's being revealed come through when we slow down enough to feel the energies that are arising to the surface. It's only through the **surrender** and the revealing of the lessons that our greatest insights come that give us the faith to believe in a path forward to overcome overwhelm.

Let's just take a moment and address the word "surrender" because it's important to note that surrendering is not giving up nor is it raising the white flag. Surrender is not about quitting. An unfortunate truth is that most of us will do anything we can to change any given moment in our lives. We eat to change how we feel, we don't like what we hear in the news so we get in debates, we always find ways to need something and it's this energy of needing that subconsciously motivates us to desire to change any given situation.

Surrendering is about acceptance. It's about understanding what is, simply is, and we cannot always change every circumstance.

Sure, in the outer world (specifically in the business landscape), we'll need to tap into that yang energy and change processes and procedures to be more profitable because, at the end of the day, businesses are in, well business, to make a profit, right? If your mind is going here, then I see you and I understand and I invite you to take a breath and step back and take another breath and feel for yourself that it's this thought that comes through that wants to challenge the words you're reading that represents this energy of desiring to change what simply is. Are you following?

If this is resonating with you and you'd like to go deeper, I did a podcast about the art of "surrendering" with Kute Blackson and you can find the episode by scanning the QR code below. Kute is a Transformational Speaker & Author of the Bestselling Book, "The Magic of Surrender". Kute is highly respected and has been endorsed by the likes of Larry King, Jack Canfield, and Marianne Williamson, to name a few, and I feel honored to have had the opportunity to interview him. This pod also explores relationships - it's so good that I've listened to it, even though I hosted it myself, several times. The code is below if you'd like to check it out.

Too often our mind plays tricks on us and wants to challenge others, forget about spiritual and religious beliefs and politics - those are big topics, let's just keep it simple for now. Have you ever noticed that when you're in conversation with another you have a thought that you want to share while they're speaking?

While conversing instead of being fully present with the other(s), our mind is already racing thinking about what we will say next, and if we're just patient enough we may be able to resist the temptation of cutting them off. This is the energy that I'm speaking to and about, and my invitation for you is to surrender to those thoughts so that you can allow them to drift through and be fully present in the moment. Personally, I love to come back to my breath when I'm in conversation with other(s) and notice my mind is racing with what to say next. I'll simply focus on inhaling through my nose and allowing my exhales to be through my nose even longer and slower than the inhales as this helps to subdue the thoughts and allow me to be more present with the other(s). It's such a subtle practice that most people won't even notice my breathing pattern. Try it out, I've shared it with many clients who have reported back how wonderfully it worked for them! Literally, as you read the following few paragraphs just focus on your inhales and elongating your exhales as you read; and you'll likely already feel the benefits.

Internal Family Systems (IFS) / Parts Work

The most useful tool I've found to help me accept and surrender to my inner world is a psychotherapy model known as Internal Family Systems (IFS) or simply "Parts Work". I like to think of this modality as if I'm the King of my inner Kingdom and my kingdom being my mind. You can be the Queen of your Queendom or whatever you want to call it, it doesn't really matter as long as the terminology resonates with you.

Take a moment to read these words then pause, close your eyes to imagine this scene we're about to create together, and then come back to these pages...

As you settle in reading this, notice your breath and begin to deepen the inhales and elongate the exhales. Imagine a kingdom in a faraway land, perhaps you're a Game of Thrones fan or a Lord of the Rings junkie, or maybe there's some other sort of kingdom that resonates with you. Begin to paint the picture with the brushstrokes from your mind's eye allowing your inner artist to come forth. What do you see?

Maybe you see rolling green hills with sunshine beaming down bright spots on parts of the land and dark shadows in some of the valleys. Maybe you see a lively village with people working, kids playing and animals in between them all amidst the rooster's crow. Maybe you see some knights rolling in on horses to the castle in which you're residing and looking out from your throne. Take a moment to just close your eyes, to see this vision, and begin to slow down your breath even more.

You have a clear vision, right?

Great, let's get into it ...

Imagine a throne, it's your throne and you're sitting in it. You are the King or Queen of this castle and the castle represents your mind. All of a sudden you hear a voice (thought) that says something to the tune of "you're not good enough, rich enough, smart enough, trustworthy enough, and good-looking enough to deserve this throne". Okay, so we hear this voice ... Let's first decide what this voice is representing. Maybe it's representing what I would call an "adversarial voice" meaning it's a thought form or a part of you that represents keeping you limited and internal turmoil. It's a part of our mind (psyche) that wants to keep us "playing small" if you will. The next step as we hear this thought form or (part of ourself), is to imagine them as a village person standing 20+ feet in front of you. They are looking up to you on your throne to voice their complaint and their opinion. Although you are the Queen or the King, they are simply coming in to voice their opinion. They are not you, they are a small part of you. Listen to what they say. As this part of you speaks its Truth to you, no need to rebuttal - all you'll respond with is a simple "Thank you".

Each time this part of you says something, you respond by saying "Thank you". As this interaction continues to unfold this thought form (part of you) begins to soften almost like it's confused. It's as if this part wanted you to get ruffled up and nervous, anxious, and confrontational but when you maintain your calm and **accept** what they have to say they begin to soften, and as they do they drift away. What's happening here is that this part (or thought form) simply desired to be seen, heard, and witnessed, and by you accepting and surrendering to what they have to say they drift on.

The next step in this process is to give this specific voice a name. For example, my adversarial voice is called "Hommy" and that's because when I was a little kid I would shout and scream saying "Hommy no Himming" which meant Sammy no Swimming. Hommy to me represents my inner child who is rebellious for the sake of being rebellious, who wants to quit, and who is always there to challenge me to see if I am ready to step up to the plate. When I notice this part of me coming through, I simply pause and slow down to hear what Hommy wants to say, and in the process of hearing him out he slowly drifts away and I'm able to move from a chaotic inner turmoil state of being to peace. Truly, I am at inner peace when I process what he or other parts of me come to the surface.

Typically you'll have 3-5 main parts of you that come to the surface and want to be seen, heard, and witnessed and the exercise in this step is to begin to build relationships with these parts and at the end of this chapter, you'll find all the details on just how to do that. Before we get there, I do want to mention that the way I teach and work with IFS or "Parts Work" is a bit different than how Richard Schwartz developed IFS and how most psychotherapists practice IFS. I've found that this slightly different version of Parts Work has helped me and my clients as it's so simple and easy to relate to. With that said, here's a bit of information about IFS so you know the basics of IFS teachings as opposed to the process I'm proposing.

The 3 main roles within the IFS framework are Managers, Exiles & Firefighters. The Manager part within us does its best to intercept feelings of intense emotions. In a sense, the Managers send these thoughts and feelings off to be Exiled. When exiled, it's similar to compartmentalization – the thought, feeling, story, etc. is put in a box not to be opened.

In daily life, when we experience a trigger, the exiled part of ourselves is activated and as that compartmentalized box is opened, the nervous system gets flushed with intense emotions ... When this happens, the Firefighter part comes to "save the day" through seeking impulsive stimulation to dissociate (avoid) these intense feelings. This process as you can see is chaotic in nature and the practice of IFS is to sit with these parts to help bring yourself back into harmony. The aim is to access the Self.

The Self is your true nature, when the parts within are allowed to have a seat at the table for tea, that is when we can find homeostasis within and the Self shines through in its peaceful nature. There's so much to be said about IFS / Parts Work, if you'd like to go deeper, check out the QR code below that will take you to a podcast I did with Alicia Kay, a licensed trauma counselor and trained in IFS work as well. If you'd like to learn even more you could go to ifs-institute.org which is the official website of IFS.

Integrate & Take Action

During any given day you may experience a trigger that sends your nervous system into fight or flight, we're well aware of this by now and to recap this is how you would apply the B.R.E.A.T.H. process...

First, **breathe** to slow down, next **relax** into it and notice the feelings arising within you, these feelings are **energies** that will be revealing something to you and now we're at the stage of **acceptance.** It can be extremely challenging to accept and surrender in this moment and for the sake of keeping this process accessible to you and so it will only take a few minutes out of your day, what I'm going to suggest you do is get to know your parts. That way, when something comes up, if it is challenging, you can step into the throne and have a conversation with one of your parts to help soften and surrender to the fleeting energy that wants to move through you.

The questions below are designed to help you get started in naming your parts. This book isn't about parts work and you can certainly go deeper, this is meant to provide you with a jumpstart so that you have the basic foundation to help guide you as you implement the B.R.E.A.T.H. process.

JOURNALING EXERCISE

What is a recurring thought or belief you have? Don't overthink it, just write.

JOURNALING EXERCISE

What is the story behind this belief? Let's get to the root of it, how is this thought form making you feel?

JOURNALING EXERCISE

Please don't overthink this one, just give this part of yourself a name.

_____

_____

_____

_____

Great work! Now you have a name for this part of you and you'll be able to step into your own inner Kingdom when this part comes in. Remember, your role is to simply hear it out, don't get lost in the story of what the part is revealing, just say "Thank you" until it drifts away and continue to focus on your breath as you sit with this part.

If you'd like to work on naming your additional parts, I'd suggest to take about 20 minutes, grab your journal and use this same process to get to know your other parts.

Additionally on the QR code below, you'll find a guided meditation where you'll be guided through a visualization to get to know your parts and in it I'll be walking you through what it feels like to step into your inner Kingdom (or Queendom).

CHAPTER 11

Step #5 - TRANSFORM into Empowering Beliefs

I BELIEVE ONE of the most toxic traits is false positivity. Now, I don't want to lose you here with this hot take because I consider myself an extremely positive person, that said, when I'm not in a good mood, when I'm facing challenges ... whatever it may be ... I will not put on a smile and lie to myself and pretend like everything is okay. Remember that shadow work is about being ruthlessly honest with yourself to have the courage to face what's rising to the surface.

Our bodies are intelligent and they speak to us in miraculous ways and when you are out of integrity with your word, your body will typically react to get your attention. It may start with what some call a "whisper" which means a small signal to let you know that the body is in dis-ease. Yet, if you ignore that signal the whisper will become a "scream" and that scream is something you can no longer ignore. What we've been doing up to this point is shadow work, and now that we've been radically honest with ourselves, it's time for the positive affirmations!

> **"** *I think it's very hard to control negative thoughts directly by trying to suppress them, but we can introduce a positive thought*
> - **Dr. Andrew Huberman**

To transmute means to change completely and not go back to the original state. Our aim has been to surrender so deeply to the energies that have been our teachers so that we can unequivocally transcend overwhelm and step into inner peace. To do this, we'll need to let go, release, and only then can we transmute negatively charged energies in the body.

Before we continue, I'd also like to address the time commitment to this whole process. I've heard so many times in my life statements like, "I wish I had more time for mindfulness" or even more alarming "I don't even have time to breathe". Remember, I'm writing this book for you; I've done my best to create this process so that it doesn't feel complicated to add to your daily routine, and in all honesty it's not! The approach I have been teaching you is about awareness. It's not about adding two 20-minute sessions of meditation a day. It's about noticing your thoughts and feelings, catching them in the moment, and reframing them and the best part is this entire process can just take a few minutes. Yet, the challenge you'll be facing is to create moment-to-moment awareness.

As we've been learning, our conscious mind only makes up 5% of our total awareness. With this in mind, the question becomes, "How would we even be able to shift our subconscious awareness to work for us in our efforts to overcome overwhelm if we're barely aware of our thoughts and feelings?"

I'll tell you how ...

Learning how to self-regulate the nervous system is the key to accessing your subconscious mind. In other words, noticing when we're in a fight or flight response and teaching our body it's safe and to shift into rest and digest more naturally when needed.

The first 4 steps of the B.R.E.A.T.H. Process are all centered around cultivating your awareness. Let's review ...

Step 1: Breathe to Slow Down

Step 2: Relax to Feel

Step 3: Energy to Reveal

Step 4: Accept to Surrender

Have you noticed a theme yet?

Each of these steps is about getting to know your internal world and it's centered around regulating your nervous system. On any given day, we may experience an overwhelming amount of stress, anxiety, panic, or even fear. That's just the nature of our reality, we have so many moving parts in the external world that all it takes is one call from your child's school, one email with bad news, or a disturbing flash of another mass shooting on your social media feed. The opportunity to feel overwhelmed is unfortunately abundant, yet the good news is we are able to take control of our thoughts and feelings should we so choose.

It's time to **transform** the energies that create overwhelm into **empowering limitless beliefs.** You are so much more powerful than you've ever known or been led to believe and I'm here to remind you of that dormant energy within you that is the co-creator of your life. Have you ever noticed that when you're in

121

a funk it seems like things only get worse? Have you noticed when you just can't get out of a negative thought loop in your head life continues to become more challenging?

When it feels like we're banging our head against the wall in frustration of things not going right and that we're swimming upstream is exactly when it's time to go within and see what our current mental state is like. Self-perpetuating negative thoughts create a negative environment in which we live. This is science. According to Science.org, quantum physics teaches that "reality is what you choose it to be". Dr. Joe Dispenza is quoted as saying, "How you think and how you feel creates your state of being".

With all of this in mind, it becomes a lightbulb moment that we are constantly creating our Reality!

(As an aide: I can see Homer Simpson's eyes wide open with this profound realization)

When you think negatively, you experience negativity in life.

When you think positively, you receive more positivity in life.

Remember too that science teaches us that we have 70,000 thoughts a day, 80% of them are from the day before and 90% of those thoughts are negative!

Now, I don't want to steer you wrong and for you to just be like, "well shoot, why do this sticky, hard, and uncomfortable shadow work when I can just feel positive all the time".

Remember what I said earlier about false positivity, that is a trap. When people avoid their shadow work and stack positive affirmations above unprocessed dense energies, they are building up more internal unprocessed negativity in the body, and at some point that pressure gets so big that it becomes too much for the body. I've had multiple clients, "busy" professionals - I'm talking multiple six-figure salary executives - collapse straight on their faces - only to wake up with bruises and bloody rips in their skin. What they were experiencing was far more than burnout. It was the 100-hour work weeks getting to them and their body responding in whispers until they couldn't ignore it anymore and the body literally shut down to awaken their inner turmoil that could be avoided no longer. Please, I urge you with my pure heart's desire, to not avoid your shadow work. It's the shadow work that releases the pent-up negative energies that creates the space for positive affirmations. Capiche?

I'm stepping down from my soap box and letting my passion for this take a back seat so that we can get practical about what this transformation actually looks like.

Say you're in a work situation and you just experienced some stress. Let's keep it simple and pretend it's an email that just came through that got your heart racing. It doesn't matter what the content of the email is - the point here is that in reading this email you are now in fight or flight. What do you do?

#1: Breathe, pause, and slow down.

#2: Relax and feel what's coming to the surface.

#3: Let the **Energies** reveal something to you.

#4: No matter how hard it is, come back to your breath and **Accept** whatever it is that is being revealed to you.

#5: Transform that lesson, story, narrative, belief, or experience into an empowering limitless belief.

It's important to note that you cannot skip step #4 of acceptance.

It can be easy to go through the first 3 steps, but skipping step #4 is not allowed per the rant above. Got it?

This entire process can literally take just 2 minutes. Remember, that science teaches us that our bodies have a 90-second physiological response when we experience an emotion, and emotions are energy in motion. So, with this in mind, really allow yourself to surrender to this energy and let it move through you. Once you do that, you ask yourself, "What is an empowering belief around this situation?"

In this example of this vague email you received that sent you in a panic like you're fighting off a saber tooth tiger but in reality ... you're sitting in your cushioned office chair staring at a computer screen with cool AC keeping your body comfortable, so remember that and get out of your mind and come back to feeling your feet on the floor getting grounded. This is the art of presence and as you breathe through the first 4 steps and ask yourself the question leading you to an empowering belief, a thought of "I am safe and supported" comes through. Don't overthink it, use that. "I am safe and supported". You breathe into this feeling of knowing that you're safe in your office and feeling supported by the chair in which you're resting your back. "I am safe and supported". Continue breathing slowly, in and out, long and slow, and repeating "I am safe and supported".

Within minutes, you're transformed. You're now feeling rested, reassured, and even confident and can move on with your day. Yet, we're not done yet and that's what step #6 is about, you'll have to take some form of action on what happened and we'll get there in the next chapter. For now, I want you to see and feel in your body how this entire process just takes a few minutes. It's not about setting aside 20 minutes for meditation and then going back to the stress and chaos of your life. It's about noticing how you feel throughout the day and catching those thoughts and feelings in real-time; it's a meditation as life if you will. It's about awareness and it's about creating your reality by not being a victim to negative energies that keep you stuck. It's within this process that you feel peace, even if it's just for a minute, you feel that peace and you become centered as you continue with this being your new mindset and approach in which you walk through life, you'll begin to retrain your subconscious to work for you as an ally in bringing more abundance and ease into your life.

With all of this being said, old habits rarely go away easily and this is when we can come back to the wisdom of Dr. Joe. He teaches what he refers to as the "Change Game" and its core philosophy is noticing when that adversarial thought comes back in and it's determined to keep you stuck. In that moment that you notice the limiting thought, simply say in your mind, "CHANGE". The purpose of saying "change" in your mind is to trigger the neural pathways in your brain to fire and wire new neural networks. Science shows that it takes repetition for your brain to build a new neural pathway. In this case, the repetition of new thoughts will help you create new, more empowering beliefs. When you say "change", you're training yourself to catch those old habits and reshape them into empowering beliefs as opposed to getting stuck in the loop of victim mentality. You may be wondering as well, "wait didn't you just say in the last chapter to surrender to these thoughts and feel them and why now are we not embracing them?" If you're thinking this, this is a great question! And to answer that question, think of this as a process of tug and pull. You will need to surrender upfront before you move on to transforming the thoughts into an empowering belief. Yet, that is not to say that the old thought form totally dissipates because in all sincerity it likely won't, but what it will do is it will soften. And when it comes back is when you say "Change". So, surrender up front and throughout your day, notice it, and say "change" when appropriate.

This is a process and have compassion with yourself as you build your awareness and realize those negative thoughts aren't the enemy. They are here to teach us and guide us because if we didn't have these negative thoughts to test us in this process, they wouldn't serve as the fuel for the fire within that is determined to create a life of more ease, joy, and abundance. Don't get mad at yourself for the negative thoughts you notice, see them as something that you now have the power to redeem and bring more positivity into your life.

This doesn't need to be hard or difficult, we can bring excitement to the process. As I notice limiting beliefs, I actually get excited because now I see it as a chance to grow even more and approach it with gratitude. Michael Jordan famously talked about fear in referring to the fear he experienced and transforming it into fuel. When I'm working with my clients, I like to guide them to ignite their own "Inner Beast" within and let this be your invitation to "Unleash the Beast". The beast being the part of ourself that we repress, let it out so it can move thoroughly (safely of course) and when those fears (or limiting beliefs) come through, let that be the fuel to ignite your fire within to stoke the flame of your determination to build the version of yourself that brought you to read this book because you know within you, you're ready for a massive transformation!

We're not done yet though as now it's time to unpack some science that will serve as the foundation to integrate limitless beliefs into your subconscious mind.

Entering Theta to Create a New Personal Reality

During the day, while we're performing normal tasks, we're operating in a beta brain wave state. There are three ranges of beta, yet for our purposes, we're not going to explore all three. We're going to keep this simple and just equate beta with "normal waking life".

Science teaches us, and I've learned through Dr. Joe's teachings specifically, that reprogramming our subconscious mind requires that we shift from beta brain waves into theta brain waves. Theta represents the doorway to the subconscious mind and as such would be to tell the subconscious mind how it is we'd like to feel and think so that it can influence our conscious awareness. So, the next obvious question is how do we make that shift?

We naturally enter theta right before we drift off to sleep and at that moment we begin to wake up, we can also enter theta through breathwork and meditation as well. It's for this reason that I've been teaching you breathwork and to call in how you want to feel when you're slowing down through your breath. This is one of the times that your brain is most receptive to receiving the signal that it's time to break the old story and create a new identity. It's not so much about knowing which brain waves are being activated – just know that when you're in a state akin to Sleep, as Neville Goddard described it, your conscious mind is less active and your subconscious is wide open, more ready to accept whatever you tell it.

Additionally, before you go to bed and when you wake up in the morning, is another great time to retrain your belief system. I would recommend one affirmation that you're working with and starting there, for 5 days you can say this affirmation when you go to bed (while you're in bed), when you wake up in the morning (still in bed), and throughout the day as needed when utilizing the B.R.E.A.T.H. process.

Integrate & Take Action

We're going to start easy here and make this just a simple 2-day challenge. Your challenge, should you choose to accept it, just kidding this isn't Mission Impossible - but seriously, please act on this ... is to create ONE Empowering Limitless Belief and repeat it in the mornings and evenings.

What are you working through most right now? Is it stress, anxiety, an old story ... What is it?

Use the B.R.E.A.T.H. process to allow the energy of what it is to reveal itself to you, surrender to it, and create a positive affirmation (AKA "Limitless Belief"), and write it down below.

Before you write it down, there's one thing I must share with you and it's that your statement will be an "I am" statement as opposed to "I will" or any form of future-based statements. The reason we will be writing in it in the present tense is because we are training your subconscious mind to **feel as** if you already have it and that is the key to manifestation. To feel it in the present moment.

As Neville Goddard put it in his book, *Feeling is the Secret*, "I AM healthy is a stronger feeling than 'I will be healthy'. To feel 'I will be' is to confess, 'I am not'. 'I am' is stronger than 'I am not'. What you feel you are always dominates what you feel you would like to be. Therefore, to be realized the wish must be felt as a state *that is* rather than a state *that is not*. Sensation precedes manifestation and is the foundation upon which all manifestation rests."

So, again, write an empowering statement below that excites you and that is in the present moment.

Great job! Now that you have your empowering limitless belief, say it out loud to yourself tonight in bed repeatedly as you drift off to sleep. Guess what you're going to do tomorrow morning? Same thing! And tomorrow evening and the next morning as well. Notice how you feel. If you'd like to change it at that point, change it and update it as you continue to integrate this into your daily life.

The last thing I'll say on this is that we are working on one statement at a time to make it more accessible for your subconscious mind to accept this as true so that you are fully committed to this one feeling. That said, I'd encourage you to use the B.R.E.A.T.H. process throughout the day and as you use this process the limitless belief you come to in your daily life may be different than the one you're using in your morning and evening routine and that is perfectly okay!

On the QR code below you'll find a link to a video where I'll be walking you through a visualization to unveil your empowering limitless belief and demonstrating how you'll be working with this new belief system.

CHAPTER 12

Step #6 - HABITS to Integrate

I LIKE TO say that, "SOUL/Life Balance is a practice because there's no end destination in sight, you're already here and there's nothing to chase". In yogic philosophy, there's a concept known as Sadhana. Sadhana means to be in pursuit of and really at its core, it's about your daily disciplines and practices (habits) that support your aim in maintaining your ultimate potential.

During my yoga teacher training, my instructor (Dakota Shae) said that "to name your ultimate potential is to limit your ultimate potential". This statement floored me ... I remember sitting on the bolster crossed legged in the yoga studio looking out of the clear glass windows behind him with the lush Costa Rican jungle immersing us and it felt as if a lightning bolt went through my system as I had this massive aha light bulb moment.

I had known I was chasing success and that's what led to my numbing depression yet it was in this moment that it now clicked with me on what to do differently. You see, I was chasing the credential to put behind my name of being named to Silicon Valley's 40 under 40 list, I was chasing the money in building a million dollar business, and in the end what I was truly chasing was external validation. I was naming my ultimate potential with these accolades and external things that I thought would bring me happiness, but it didn't.

Now, I no longer name my ultimate potential and instead I focus on the daily habits that bring me joy and inner peace and that's what this final step of the B.R.E.A.T.H. process is all about. It's about the **habits** you'll be **integrating** into your daily life because if you don't make changes in your daily routine then it'll be next to impossible to experience the transformation you've been seeking. Specifically in our case it's about making the habits to overcome the debilitating overwhelming feelings that come in and out throughout the day.

In my early days of building my business, my approach was to "start with the end in mind" and "reverse engineer" from there to reach my goal. While this mindset and process absolutely work, I would suggest making a slight shift in how we perceive this approach. That shift is that the end in mind isn't about an end destination nor is it about achieving a specific goal. The end in mind is how we want to feel and in truth, we don't actually need to wait to achieve something for an end result of a feeling. We can access the feeling we're calling in simply through our habits and routines that support our "ultimate potential".

Dr. Andrew Huberman teaches that high performers avoid the crashes associated with burnout because they attach dopamine to the effort process. As Dr. Huberman said himself, "dopamine is not just about reward ... dopamine is about motivation and drive. It's like a jet that propels you along the path". It's important to be working on projects, whether it's personal development, creative outlets, business endeavors, or anything else that resonates with you, and my hope is that you see that what's even more important is the process rather than the destination. It's in the process itself that not only brings greater fulfillment, but also with the release of dopamine, it helps to keep us on the right path.

JOURNALING EXERCISE

In the lines below, write a few words or a sentence about how you would like to feel. Would you like to feel more at peace, more joyful, more playful, more loving? ... How is it **you** would like to feel?

Great, good work!

This is your desired feeling that we're calling in and another thing to note is that we must notice if there's a chasing or a needing energy around this feeling. Firstly, If you notice you may be chasing (or even needing) this feeling, the challenge is that you're now playing a game in which we could refer to as "the lack game". You're approaching it as though it's a carrot on a stick and you'll find yourself running in circles like a hamster on a wheel.

Secondly, if there's a subconscious story of lack, you're telling yourself "I am not that" and in doing so you're repelling what it is you're asking to feel. But the best part about all of this is that the thing you're desiring is a feeling, which means it is always accessible within you. So, rather instead when you are writing down the desired feeling you're calling in, it's important to understand that you can feel that energy right now and you can do so through the B.R.E.A.T.H. process, and here's how it would look in real-time...

You just received a notice that you have a big bill due and you're currently short on cash, what do you do?

Well, for most of us, our inner world will begin to shift into fight or flight and as so we hold our breath and now we're in a state of panic. But, for a fleeting moment, you remembered that book you're reading about overcoming overwhelm and you consciously chose to use the B.R.E.A.T.H. process and this is what will happen for you...

You begin to notice your **breath** and take **slow** inhales through your nose and allow your exhales to be even longer than your inhales. As you continue to breathe in this way, you begin to **relax** and in doing so you allow yourself to **feel** the panic rising to the surface. The panic and inner turmoil are an **energy** that began to **reveal** something to you and as you continue to breathe through these feelings you realize that you grew up in a household that was always fearful of not having enough money to make ends meet and thus a story was implanted in your psyche from your youth that not having money equates to feeling panicked. Whereas in the past, you would have let this feeling ruminate for the rest of your evening, gone to bed with this feeling, and awaken still feeling it, this time you choose a different path ... you choose to accept the feeling of panic and surrender to the fear implanted in your subconscious mind for a lifetime. As your heart rate continues to slow down and you breathe through this unwelcome feeling you notice that you are beginning to shift into a restful state. It's in this moment that you **transform** the fear into the **empowering belief** of "I have everything I need at this moment and I am safe". As you breathe this affirmation into your being, your subconscious mind receives the message, the cells of your body hear that you're safe and you begin to feel inner peace thus transforming the panic into peace.

This example is something we can all relate to because the fear of money (or lack thereof) is deeply ingrained in our collective subconscious minds. If it were not a place of contention, we wouldn't trade our time for money because in Truth we do spend the majority of our day (and therefore) our lives working. Not that working is bad and that we don't enjoy the work we do, but at the end of the day most people (whether or not they love their jobs) are working to make money as money is a necessity to live and meet Maslow's basic hierarchy of needs.

That said, money isn't something to be fearful about, sure sometimes the bills stack up and literally we don't know how we're going to pay them off. I'll tell you one thing I know for sure ... worrying and panicking is not going to get you to a solution, solutions come from a clear and grounded approach.

It's in the B.R.E.A.T.H. process that you have the ability to shift into a level-headed mindset at any given moment and it starts with the choice to engage with the process. This entire process can take as little as 2 minutes. Seriously, you don't need a 20-minute meditation to feel bliss, what you need is to let go of your negative thoughts by allowing yourself to feel them and the breath is the access point to surrender to them so that they can move through you and you can transform them into thoughts and feelings that do serve you.

On the other hand, I'm a practical guy and understand that taking a couple of minutes out of your day to shift your feeling state doesn't necessarily solve the issue at hand. This is where the "H" in the B.R.E.A.T.H. process comes into play ... **habits** to **integrate**. In our example of a bill that needs to be paid, what are we going to do about it?

You must find first a solution for this one specific bill and secondly (and I'd argue) more importantly create new habits that you can integrate into your life so that this doesn't happen again. Maybe, in this situation, the solution is to sell stocks or if you have to open a new 0% credit card, ask friends and family for support, or something else, there's always a solution if you're resourceful enough and to get resourceful we need to come from a grounded approach, not a state of panic.

Secondly, new habits are required, this is more important so that you don't get yourself in this situation again, and this can be a variety of things to do from checking your bank account daily or weekly, to creating (and sticking to) a new budget, or using an online service that helps to identify subscriptions so that you can cancel the ones you don't need or have forgotten about.

The point is that you're just going to come back again and again, month after month, year after year, with the same old stories and narratives that have kept you in an overwhelming state of being which we now know is just a signal for a deeper underlying condition of your psyche and/or unprocessed emotions and even traumas. That is, if you don't make the changes in your daily life of new habits and that first new habit I would encourage you to embody is connecting to your breath. It's as simple as noticing your breath when you're speaking with another, be more present with what it is they are saying rather than being lost in your mind by just noticing your inhales and elongating your exhales.

By adopting this approach, you'll begin to re-shape the way you breathe so that you notice all the times throughout your day you hold your breath. And as you continue to do this, you'll also notice that you are feeling less overwhelmed throughout the day because you're subtly shifting from fight or flight to rest and digest.

Carl Jung has been quoted as saying, "I am not what happened to me, I am what I choose to become. You are what you do, not what you say you'll do". The question I have for you is, are you ready to choose who you are becoming? It's a daily choice and the mastery comes in noticing moment to moment how you're choosing to be and feel.

Integrate & Action

Consistent action is all that matters, so let's make it easy on ourselves and not add to the overwhelm by making this accessible. My vision for you is that tomorrow you'll really notice just once when you're holding your breath and in that noticing, you'll begin to shift into deeper inhales and exhales. Maybe you apply the B.R.E.A.T.H. process to a situation tomorrow or maybe it comes the next day ... or the following day. But, in the next three days, definitely find a time to apply the B.R.E.A.T.H. process and stay committed to noticing your thoughts and feelings and working with these subtle shifts that just take a couple of minutes. I promise you that if you commit to this, 3 months from now, you'll be a totally different person. Your friends, your family, your colleagues ... literally everyone will notice it and they'll be able to tell because we are energetic beings and you'll be leading from a more balanced energy that is palpable and contagious (in a very very positive way).

Just imagine, if your workplace was an environment where everyone had the tools to regulate their nervous system in this fashion, imagine if all your vendors and clients felt this way, imagine if everyone in your home felt this way, imagine if you could interact with your parents and/or your children in this way and finally imagine if everyone on the planet was able to slow down and process their feelings. The world as a whole, would shift, would it not?

So, let's make this easy and let's make it fun, here's your final assignment as part of the 6-step B.R.E.A.T.H. process.

Checking in with Yourself

Set your alarm clock for 12pm tomorrow and in your alarm, write "Breathe for 2 minutes". By setting your alarm and giving it a title, you're making it as easy as possible to remind yourself to just take a moment to slow down, to feel, and let those energies reveal anything that's coming through, and if they are heavier feelings, remember to accept them and finally to transmute them into a positive affirmation. It's a simple assignment, very easy ... just breathe.

JOURNALING EXERCISE

In the lines below, jot down some actions that have come up for you throughout reading these 6 steps. What new changes are you ready to commit to? If you're feeling stuck, read over the list of ideas above and choose some new habits...

Earlier in this step we explored the purpose behind Sadhana and now it's time for you to create some daily practices that you can integrate into your life. Everything you've done up from this point is just 10% of the work. The real transformation and overcoming of the overwhelm lies within the integration of what you've learned, identified, and practiced thus far. The practice is that of awareness, of coming back to yourself again and again and as you continue to practice you'll build greater moment-to-moment consciousness. This is literally how you bring the 95% of your subconscious (unknown) awareness to conscious awareness. Think of it as a muscle and the more you commit to your Sadhana the greater awareness you'll have.

In an effort to help kickstart you on the process, below is a QR code that will take you to a 5-Day Challenge to help you create new habits and shatter limiting beliefs.

CHAPTER 13

Your Road Map for the Path Ahead

"LIFE IS GONNA life" and in the ebbs and flows of the experience of being a human we're undoubtedly going to experience overwhelm. That's the thing about this journey, there isn't a destination to land upon in which we'll be in an ongoing state of inner peace. Rather, when the waves of overwhelm come crashing to the shores of your inner landscape, that is when the B.R.E.A.T.H. Process will serve you best. At its core the B.R.E.A.T.H. Process is simple, yet it's in the practical application that it becomes nuanced.

The very first step is to have the intention to heal and by heal I mean to make the conscious decision to enter in the shadows of your psyche to transmute feelings and emotions that are easily suppressed. The access point to healing is through your breath, which is why the very first step is to just breathe. Connecting to your breath is the foundation upon which everything else can be built.

When we're experiencing overwhelm, it's easy to get stuck in the fight or flight response, so as you breathe; remember that you want to relax into it. The aim is to shift from fight or flight into rest and digest and we can do so by softening. Long and slow inhales and even longer and slower exhales will be the key to relaxation so that you can feel what's rising to the surface.

After relaxing and beginning to enter into the para-sympathetic nervous system, you'll start to be more aware of the energies you're encountering on a daily basis. This includes your own energy, the energy of others, and the energy of everything you come into contact with.

These energies are all here to teach you something and when you get curious, you can begin to see how these energies are revealing something for you to look at. One of the hardest things about shadow work is surrendering to what simply "is". Often we want to change something about ourselves, another, or anything in the outside world. Yet, the paradox is that the only way we can change is through acceptance.

When you truly accept and surrender to the feelings and emotions arising within is also when you're ready to transmute them and transform into the version of yourself you previously were chasing. Maybe it's more confidence, perhaps more inner peace, or maybe it's just being more aware of your thoughts and feelings throughout the day.

Finally, we have habits. All of this work will be in vain if you do not find a way to integrate new habits and ways of being into your daily life.

Below is a summary of the 6-Step B.R.E.A.T.H. Process.

BREATHE to Slow Down
RELAX to Feel
ENERGY to Reveal
ACCEPT to Surrender
TRANSFORM into Empowering Beliefs
HABITS to Integrate

What I hope you remember when you experience a trigger or an emotion that you normally wouldn't want to feel is 3 simple things ... First, breathe, secondly feel and lastly think intentionally. These 3 simple phases summarize each of the steps within the 6-Step B.R.E.A.T.H. Process.

Now, there's also another tidbit of information I haven't shared with you quite yet and that is the benefits of daily habits.

List of Tools for Daily Habits

Healthy habits are crucial to moving beyond overwhelm, below are just a few habits you may want to consider to help improve your mental well-being, emotional state, and overall feeling good in your body.

- **Sunlight first thing in the morning:** this is such a great practice! Getting sunlight first thing in the morning gets you outside and the sun reduces melatonin which helps you feel more awake throughout the day, reduces cortisol levels (stress), and helps improve sleep quality.
- **Movement:** I'm partial to yoga, but anything that resonates with you whether it's weight lifting, swimming, pickleball, running, cycling, surfing, stretching ... you name it. Are you currently getting in your body daily? And I'm not suggesting working out every day, it can be as simple as adopting a new morning and evening routine to feel into your body.
- **Mental Toughness:** Hold / Cold therapy through the use of cold plunges stacked with the sauna has been a game changer for my mental health! There are a lot of resources out there that speak to the benefits and how to get started to build mental fortitude.

- **Breathwork Routines:** Exercises like the cyclic sigh or box breathing are a great place to start, just remember that on a daily basis, we want to utilize breathwork exercises that activate rest and digest while we'll save the deep dives of breathwork journeys for when we are ready for a massive release.

- **Water:** Are you getting enough water? I follow the advice of drinking half of my body weight (in ounces) per day. So for me, I'm targeting a little less than 100 ounces of water per day and I notice the days I drink more water how much better I feel. Pro Tip: Start your day (before coffee) with a glass of water.

- **Healthy Eating Habits:** Before meals, find gratitude for the food you're about to consume. When you notice you may be binge snacking, slow down and breathe, give yourself 90 seconds to feel rather than to consume to avoid and/or numb what you're feeling.

- **Journaling:** How do you feel when you journal? Do you find it helpful? If you find yourself saying you don't have the time to journal, maybe look up the "5 Minute Journal", it's a great companion book that I've used in the past that is geared towards "busy professionals" who believe they don't have time to journal.

- **Creative Outlets:** How are you expressing your creativity? I've gotten into painting and for me, this artistic expression has unlocked so much. Where can you let your inner artist out?

- **Play:** How are you bringing play into your life? We tend to take things way too seriously, what brings the playful side of you out and how can you do more of that to bring more play into your life?

- **Meditation:** We haven't covered meditation much and that's because there are plenty of resources for meditation and this book is centered around breathwork, yet meditation offers profound benefits. At the time of writing this book, I established a 10-minute breathwork and meditation routine. It's very simple and very calming to the nervous system and accessible for anyone no matter how hard time is to come by. Simply do 5 minutes of breathwork to settle the mind and let that lead into 5 minutes of stillness (meditation).

- **Music**: Below you'll find a QR code that will take you to a playlist I made to help me reprogram my subconscious mind. I'm a fan of reggae, so, I'll let you know upfront that all of these songs are within the reggae genre. If you check out this playlist, you'll notice that many of the lyrics touch on topics within this book. One of the songs on the playlist is by Grammy award-winning band, Soja. The song is called "Press Remix" and check out these lyrics ... "then I started dreaming 'bout the future of my life. I can be anything I told myself every single night. So when I lay me down to sleep ... it's only one thing that is following me". Remember how we went over when you go to sleep your brain wave states are in Theta? Well, when your brain is in the Theta state, the subconscious mind is most receptive to change which is why this is a great time to say your affirmations. I think you'll find, if you check out this playlist, that many of these songs will reinforce what you've learned within this book and all of them are very positive and uplifting. When I start my days listening to a few songs from this playlist, the positive energy tends to carry with me throughout the day and I hope this playlist has the same effect for you as well!

Evening Reflections

Sometimes our days just get too jam-packed and for whatever reason, you just will not have the energy to lean into the heavier emotions that normally you would avoid feeling. What this could look like is experiencing stress at some point in your day and literally your adversarial voice will come in to play a game with you and tell you you don't have time to process that stress. Although we now know that processing the stress could take as little as 90 seconds if you choose to implore the 6-Step B.R.E.A.T.H. Process, none of us are perfect and sometimes you will give in to the adversarial voice and go back to temporarily distracting yourself from feeling and processing your emotions in real-time. When this happens, it's important to do a review of your day as part of your evening routine. It can be as simple as lying in bed and asking yourself where in the day you experienced emotions that you didn't process. As situations arise, simply replay the scenario, feel back into the emotion you felt then and now go through the 6-Steps so that you can clear out those energies and they don't get stuck in your body. This will help you to get a more restful night's sleep and feel more clear in the morning.

The Dark Night of the Soul

All of this is to say that sometimes we're just "in it" and it's going to take much longer than a few minutes to process the energies. By "in it" I mean that we're in the denser and heavier energies for an extended period of time. In spiritual circles, some may refer to this as "The Dark Night of the Soul".

The Dark Night of the Soul can be misleading because it has nothing to do with "a night". The Dark Night has everything to do with going through a period (or season) of your life where it's like you're being guided to sit with heavier emotions for an extended period of time. For many people, it may last several days, for others weeks, and in extreme cases months or even years. The important thing to realize about a Dark Night is that we can't force our way out of it. In many ways, we can use the 6-Step B.R.E.A.T.H. Process as a means to be "in it" yet at the same time it's not about processing emotions in 90 seconds. It's a zoomed-out version of the 6-Steps because each step of the process may take days, weeks, or perhaps months to be "in".

For example, prior to writing this book, I hit a new rock bottom, and for the purposes of sharing the practicality of how to utilize the 6-Steps the details of why I was there are not relevant. With that said, here is how I applied the 6-Steps when I recently hit a new bottom (or Dark Night).

Step #1: Breathe to Slow Down

Initially I was in resistance, there were many days when I didn't want to "do the work" and allowed myself the grace to not judge myself for eating bad food, watching movies, and temporarily numb myself. Side note, I'm a huge proponent of allowing yourself to temporarily "numb" and "distract" yourself through unconscious practices yet only for 3 days. After numbing myself for more than 3 days, it's now a new state of being and that's when I tap into my Yang energy and "Unleash the Beast" within to help motivate myself to get out of it. So in this case, I gave myself 3 days to literally eat food I normally wouldn't, lay on the couch for hours on end watching movies, and just be "in it" without trying to "fix it".

When those 3 days were up, I adopted a "Game Time" / "Let's Go" mentality and got back into my conscious and intentional practices which included breathwork as a foundational element. That's not to say I was "cured" and "healed", I was very much still in the Dark Night, only now, I was letting go of the victim mentality and was "leaning in" to the work that needed to be "in it" so I could "move through it".

Step #2: Feel to Relax

With this example, remember that this was a process that took several days, so it wasn't like I would notice an emotion and go through the 6-Steps, it was more like I would notice the emotions all the time because I was always feeling them and as I did feel them, I would also allow myself to relax into them. It's important when we extend the steps to apply them to a Dark Night to realize the feeling step is much more uncomfortable. It's not about breathing through a feeling for a few minutes. Sure that absolutely helps, yet then again in the next hour or so you may already have another wave of feelings come through and will need once again to process the new set of energies coming through you that don't belong to remain in you.

Step #3: Energy to Reveal

The way to reduce the amount of times you will need to feel your feels is through getting curious and being honest with yourself about what the energies are revealing to you. This step is all about getting curious and having fun with it, look for a lesson. In my example here, I had just gotten back from Bali and without getting into all of the details I felt like a failure, I felt like I had been gifted an opportunity to lean into a deeper level of shadow work and that I resisted it and ran from it. So, in following these first 3 steps I was finally able to get unstuck because in step 3 now I finally understood why I was feeling so terrible whereas before I was just feeling bad and couldn't necessarily point my finger to why I was feeling so off, down and honestly depressed with voices of "you're a phony, you're a failure, you messed that up, you're not good enough" etc. Now, I understood why I was "off", it was because, on a subconscious level, I was ashamed of myself.

Step #4: Accept to Surrender

When I finally got to this point of acceptance, I felt a weight lifted off of me ... I felt what many would call "light" and that's because I was able to release these denser energies that weren't serving me. Step number 4 is so much easier when you get really honest with yourself in the previous lesson about the lesson coming through.

Step #5: Transform into Empowering Beliefs

Now was the time for me to reignite the "Beast Within" and come back to all the times in my life when I was proud of myself to show myself that those limiting voices before were not my true authentic self. It's so much easier to give yourself a kickstart in overcoming the overwhelming negative voices when you can revisit past times in your life that bring you pride with how you showed up for yourself. As I went deeper in this stage a new mission and vision of how I want to show up for myself and the world at large came through. It was so inspiring that I literally went from rock bottom to soaring like an eagle to new heights.

Step #6: Habits to Integrate

Writing became my medicine, I realized that I had gotten away from my journaling practice and so was beginning to write to help process traumatic events that occurred the year previous. I was listening to a "Huberman Lab" podcast (episode entitled "A Science-Supported Journaling Protocol to Improve Mental & Physical Health") where he was describing a journaling exercise to help you process traumatic events. The protocol is called "Pennebaker Writing" (or "Expressive Writing") and is to write about the same traumatic/challenging event for 4 days in a row. You can listen to his podcast for more details about this. I've done this writing protocol a few years previously as I learned about it through a teacher of mine, Erick Godsey, and it really helped so I decided to go back to this exercise.

After going through this journaling protocol, I had the message of writing about these experiences in 2023 as a fiction book loosely based on the happenings and challenges of my life the year before. So, I started watching a MasterClass on how to write fiction books because all 5 of my previous books were non-fiction and I didn't know the first thing about writing a fiction book. Within a week of beginning to write that book, I paused because this book you're reading now, "Overcome the Overwhelm" wanted to be birthed. Literally, I wrote more than half of the book you're reading now in just a couple of weeks. It was like something was unlocked within me and the words just came out of me and onto the pages without even trying.

During this time some of the other habits I started to integrate included morning breathwork followed by meditation and a cold plunge along with eating healthier and a solid yoga routine.

I'm sharing all of this with you because my aim with this book is to give you the tools to catch your emotions in real-time to process them. I hope that you feel by now that this isn't about adding anything to your day. It's not about adding 20 minutes of meditation twice a day, it's not about yoga, and it's not about anything else that you'll need to carve out more time to do. Honestly, what it's about is moment-to-moment awareness and allowing yourself to go through the 6 steps within minutes so that you can process emotions in real time!

Meanwhile, this human experience is full of highs and lows, while the 6-Steps can and will help you to relieve stress and anxiety with ease on a daily basis also know that if you're feeling like you're in a funk (or a "Dark Night"), you can apply the 6-Steps from a zoomed out lens to help you move through the Dark Night and into your next Breakthrough!

In summary, remember to BREATHE.

CHAPTER 14

The Rise of Compassionate Leadership

BUT HOW CAN you, as a leader in the workplace, begin to put all of this into action? How can you not only overcome overwhelm on an individual level but create a more compassionate workplace overall? The secret to creating a more mindful, compassionate, and safe workplace is that it starts and ends with you!

It's the simple pauses between bites of food. It's slowing down to chew the dense nutrients and noticing the mouth-watering flavors and how they make you feel. It's remembering to breathe, in and out, as you bless the food that's going into your body. To close your eyes and feel the energetic charge of the gift it is to be able to taste these wonderful sensations that fill your body with vibrancy and energy.

Overcoming overwhelm is about coming back to your senses to find presence within yourself. To find (and access) inner peace, even if just a moment of inner peace. Feel that, and lead with stoic confidence as it's magnetic.

This is how we take charge and create a workplace that truly values psychological safety.

In writing this book, I really got deep with myself to do my own self-inventory of what matters to me most, why I'm writing this book and what I see for the future of how we conduct ourselves by relating to people in all their humaneness, especially infusing this heart-centered approach within the business climate. As I went deeper into this self-reflection, my new mission and vision was illuminated and I'd like to take this opportunity to share it with you.

My mission is to teach the tools to OVERCOME OVERWHELM through the practice of SOUL/Life Balance and I'm here to encourage the rise of COMPASSIONATE Leadership and eradicate the glorification of "Hustle Culture".

My vision is to move beyond "checking the box" of basic mindfulness practices in business and teach high performers how to become COMPASSIONATE Leaders in the workplace. It's to bridge the gap between Mental Health & Workplace Culture by reframing Work/Life Balance to the philosophy of SOUL/Life Balance. The 6-Step B.R.E.A.T.H. process teaches you how to overcome overwhelm through SOUL/Life Balance.

I read these mission and vision statements every single morning to keep the light of the flame within burning so strongly that the flame within can be felt in my core to guide me in my actions using this purpose as a north star.

Do you resonate with this vision? Do you also believe it's time to put an end to the glorification of "Hustle Culture"?

The unfortunate Truth is around 3 in 5 workers report they don't talk about their stress levels because they don't want to burden others. We must find ways to bridge the gap between mental health advocacy and workplace culture and create a workplace where people feel empowered to share how they feel.

It's shocking to me, yet it isn't, that 61% of workers said that people around them just expect them to get over their stress (per the American Psychological Association AKA APA).

Silently suffering has become the norm as 47% of people report that they wish they had someone to help them manage their stress! How is this okay?!

We need to throw a lifeline, and by embodying Compassionate Leadership yourself first, you will be more equipped to serve others.

This book is about overwhelm, right? Well, 36% of adults said they don't know where to start when it comes to managing their stress. Sounds like our society is overwhelmed with overwhelm?

The 6-Step B.R.E.A.T.H. Process has been specifically designed to solve this problem. Breathe, Relax, Energy, Accept, Transform, Habits ... remember this when you feel overwhelmed, embody this, and share this framework!

There is a way through and by accessing our breath and allowing what comes through to come through, we can transform it into an empowering belief and create new habits that will guide you to overcome the overwhelm!

3 Essential Tools for a Psychologically Safe Workplace

Let's get into some practical ways to transform a workplace culture to go beyond checking the box of addressing mental health.

#1. Holding Space: Earlier in the book, we spoke about holding space, revisit this section and make sure you're clear on how to hold space for yourself and others.

#2 The W.I.F.L.E.: This acronym stands for What I Feel Like Expressing. Creating a few minutes before a meeting to allow for check-ins goes a long way in creating a psychologically safe space. There's a lot more to be said about how to conduct a W.I.F.L.E. and I go over this in my Keynotes, Workshops, and Compassionate Leadership Coaching frameworks; that said here's what you need to know...

First, create and hold space, and invite those feeling like they may want to share to do so (not forcing everyone to do so), the invitation is to allow people to share in 90 seconds or less if there's anything that's keeping them from being fully present. Voicing if there is something helps free up the mental bandwidth in the mind as it also gives others a chance to see them and feel the compassion within the room. This sets a tone for a more human-to-human meeting and deeper connections which also leads to enhanced performance with all parties involved.

#3: Active Listening & Say Backs: This is an exercise I offer in corporate mindfulness workshops and one that I teach to my compassionate leadership coaching clients. The foundation of this is that we are working with a set of questions (prompts) and there are at least two people involved at a time. One person asks the question, while the other has 5 minutes to respond. The person asking the question simply says "Thank You for sharing".

The next step involves what is commonly referred to as reflections or "say backs". A say back is when the person asking the question says "What I hear you saying is ..." and they go on to reflect what they've heard. This exercise is an amazing tool to slow down our minds, be more present with one another, and experience effective mindful communication.

The bottom line is we must put in the work for ourselves first and only from there will we be able to show up as our best-embodied Self to create a ripple effect within the office, our families, and the "small" everyday encounters.

If you're serious about becoming a Compassionate Leader and applying the tools you've learned about in this book, you may want to consider joining the "SOUL/Life Breath Club". The Breath Club is a place for "busy professionals" to connect in the community to share the best tools and practices to create a more mindful workplace culture. Every week participants gather together to learn about different tools and are guided through a variety of breathwork exercises to move stuck energy while applying the 6-Step B.R.E.A.T.H. process. You can find out more about the Breath Club on the QR code below if you're interested.

You are the bridge between the version of your current culture and what you know your workplace culture can turn into! Continue with your inner work and keep shining your bright light and you will see things shift and fold to mold and reflect your inner world, trust in that.

CHAPTER 15

Just Breathe

THE SECRET TO overcoming overwhelm, if you haven't figured it out, is to surrender and accept the overwhelm. Remember this is the cosmic joke, the grand paradox if you will. There's actually nothing to overcome. It's not an obstacle. The truth is the overwhelming feeling is a signal that something is off and that's okay! We don't always need to feel great, amazing, happy, blissful, etc. We can get lost in the trap of chasing ecstatic feelings and in the process dissociate from how we feel to pretend all is great and put on a happy state and wear the mask of false positivity.

When we're experiencing overwhelm, it's an invitation to surrender to the overwhelming feeling and in surrendering to it we move through it and transform. On the flip side, if we act like the overwhelm isn't there and pretend everything is great, we are not only lying to ourselves but also creating more disharmony and inner turmoil, and as such this can lead to a whole host of disease within the body.

The narrative or rather the mindset of seeing it as something to change is what is actually keeping one stuck.

We can't change what simply is ...

When one finally stops resisting the overwhelming feelings is actually paradoxically the same time when the metamorphosis journey begins. It's the surrendering to "what is" that allows the caterpillar to crystallize and take shape and transform into the butterfly. Such is the experience with our lives as well.

Our cocoon isn't physical, instead, it's our inner world that sets the stage for transformation yet to come.

The process is simple, we just tend to overcomplicate it, and that's okay! Let's agree that we will not get lost in the victim mentality of "why do I make it so hard?". Just accept that we make it hard from time to time, then find the humor in it all. When you can get to the profound realization for yourself that it really is "all so simple" is precisely when you will feel within your core essence the simplicity of overcoming overwhelm.

It's within this surrendering to what it is, feeling it, letting it go, affirming a new belief, and making a commitment to integrate necessary changes within your life is when you'll find true and authentic gratitude. It's this exact process that will allow you to feel the overwhelm fully so that you can let it go.

Let it land in your body. Connect with your breath. Breathe into the energy that is stuck and wants to be in motion because remember emotions are energy in motion and when we don't feel our emotions that energy gets stuck and stored within the body.

Overcoming overwhelm, at its core, is about **slowing down.** The outer world moves fast, and if we put our focus there, we will let It dictate our inner world, and thus our inner world will be a landscape of chaos. So, instead, start with your inner world.

You have the ability to slow down your thoughts, your physical actions and to fully feel the energies that come in and out of your inner world.

When you notice an emotion, it's as simple as the following...

- Remember the 90-Second Rule
- Keep in mind that Emotions are Energy in Motion

AND follow these 3 Basic Principles to Overcome Overwhelm:

1. **BREATHE**
2. **FEEL**
3. **THINK INTENTIONALLY**

Start with calming inhales and exhales and begin to notice how you physically move through the world. Are you rushing from one thing to the next? Just notice, for example, if you are putting away dishes, cooking, cleaning ... any of these things, how fast are you moving? Can you slow down to be more present and make intentional moves with your body? For example, I've noticed that when I type, or say when I'm vacuuming, or even folding laundry; I'll notice my movements are fast. As soon as I have that awareness, if I can come back to my breath and slow it down through a big inhale through my nose and a longer and slower exhale, then my movements begin to slow down. As I begin to slow down physically, my mind begins to slow down and that is an easy way to shift us into presence. And it's in presence when we're not dwelling on the past nor are we imagining the future, that is when we can truly access inner peace.

Have patience, and remind yourself, there's nowhere to go, you're already here. Let this be your metaphorical permission slip to stop rushing and chasing to the next thing. Just take a deep and slow inhale and feel the energy as you slowly release your breath. You're doing great, I'm proud of you, and more importantly; I hope you are proud of yourself.

In one final moment of transparency, I'd like to share a short story with you to demonstrate how overwhelm comes into our lives, how easy it is to disregard the overwhelm, and how resisting overwhelm actually creates *more* overwhelm.

The first half of this book just flew through me, it was like I didn't even have to think about it at all. The words just came flying out of my head and my fingers were rushing to get the thoughts out of my head faster than I could type (and I'm a fast typer). That said, writer's block eventually did come for me and I took some time away from the book and this project as a whole to let the teachings from this book "breathe". Well, when I finally came back to the book and committed to getting it done, overwhelm came for me big time.

Before I knew it my calendar was stacked with calls and obligations from sunrise to past sunset, and sometimes with obligations ending as late as 8pm. I had committed to new opportunities to facilitate breathwork and teaching mindfulness practices that were in alignment with the difference I wanted to make in the world but at the expense of my own mental health. I shamed and guilted myself for not being creatively in tune with the energy needed to finish this book. This went on for almost two weeks (maybe longer).

All of this culminated in one week of back-to-back meetings all day every day where I finally felt yet once again what it feels like to "not be able to breathe". Literally, a month or so before this I received an email from a client saying something to the effect of them being so busy they wished they had time to breathe. When I received that email I was disappointed at the state of our business culture that we prioritize working so much more than our own mental health. Receiving that email lit a new fire in me to write this book. Yet, now ironically, I was the one feeling like I couldn't breathe. What had happened was for a short while I didn't follow my own advice. I let the obligations dictate my life, I let the yang energy of the outer world consume me and disregarded my thoughts and feelings.

The point of this story is that no one is perfect and my rule of thumb is that when someone is trying to put on a facade of perfection, it is exactly the same time when my B.S. radar goes off. So, please understand that this is a process. There will be times when you feel like everything you're learning to overcome stress and anxiety just clicks. You'll feel like you're riding a never-ending cosmic wave with dolphins swimming alongside you to encourage you to truly feel happy and bliss. Yet, like all things, the only constant is change and waves eventually do "break". When the ride ends, know that it's not actually ending. It's a lull between the next set and in peak performance circles this would be called the recovery stage between flow states.

No one's perfect and all we can do is be honest with ourselves. If you're in a lull, let yourself be in the lull without shaming yourself. Fully be in it so that you can feel it, release it, and transform it and at that point, it's time to call in positive thinking and feelings and take action to integrate new habits to take yourself to even higher levels!

You can do this, you already have all the tools within you, and now, you know how to put them to use.

Thank you for investing in yourself and in doing so committing to creating a world with greater connection between all of its inhabitants. The world is better off just by you simply putting your energy into self-development.

If you'd like to go deeper into your own work *and* promoting a compassionate workplace, I offer a monthly Breath Club membership, keynotes and workshops, breathwork journeys for teams, and 1:1 Compassionate Leadership coaching, found at SamKabert.com

Remember ...

Just Breathe,
Sam

ACKNOWLEDGEMENTS

I'd like to take a moment and extend my sincere gratitude to the team behind-the-scenes that helped to make this book a reality!

First and foremost, years ago (like back in 2017), I often was asked "How are you able to do so much?" The answer to that question was simple ... virtual assistants. I've built my career off match-making the right people in certain roles to support the vision - there's absolutely no way I could do any of this on my own! We are all in this together and when we tap into our own unique gifts and merge them together the outcome becomes a rich, fulfilling experience that everyone around us can enjoy as well.

With that being said, I've been working with Sushma for over 7 years now as my lead graphic designer, and along with her, I have Franz, my video editor, and Genevieve, my website designer, all to thank as they have seen the shifts over the years and have been wonderful freelancers to support the mission!

Two newer team members are Alicia Wilcox and Amy Smith. Alicia has been a pleasure to work with in editing this book and being extremely supportive in backing the mission! Amy is a friend who works in PR and has eagerly jumped on board to help with getting this book out there through various news outlets (both local and globally) and her enthusiasm and passion for the topics and message of this book keep me inspired to show up as the fullest version of myself.

One of my best friends, Celeste, saw something in me that I didn't see and she brought me into her deep healing breathwork-inspired journeys. I am forever grateful for our friendship and the lessons and experiences I've learned through her mentorship and friendship.

Megan McAllister, the owner of Pleasure Point Yoga, was the one who led and encouraged me to do a yoga teacher training despite me not having any interest in teaching yoga. That changed during my training, and when I came home and graduated, Megan gave me a rotation teaching yoga and leading a men's group at her studio which was the beginning of stepping into a leadership role in a new and more impactful way than ever before.

When I started writing this book, I knew I wanted a framework that would stick and that's when one of my mentors, Bill G. Williams (AKA Electric Bill), and I hopped on Zoom. Within minutes Bill helped lead me through a simple exercise and BOOM the 6-Step B.R.E.A.T.H. Process was born!

Last year I was on the phone with a friend of mine, Barrie Robinson, and as she was listening to how I've persevered despite the challenges I was facing, she said "this is what your next book could be about". Although at the time, it was almost a throwaway comment, now having completed this book, I see how the seed was planted in my subconscious and it warms my heart to relive that conversation with her as I was walking on the beach sharing the current happenings in my life.

Joshua Evans, Ryan Estis, Seth Mattison, and the Impact-Eleven community as a whole have all been invaluable mentors and allies in my pursuit of sharing the message of "SOUL/Life Balance" and "Overcoming Overwhelm" on stage so that these visions I have can start to have a ripple effect with an even bigger impact.

Much of my knowledge of the topics I've brought into this book has been directly correlated with my trainings in Somatic Breathwork and Bridget & Dakota Shae's Yoga Teacher Training.

My parents have been so incredibly emotionally supportive during the past several years of my life. Well, I mean my entire life, of course. Yet, 5 years ago I sat my parents down to tell them all about my first experience with the plant medicine Ayahuasca. I remember a conversation in the kitchen a few years later where my Dad asked me something to the effect of "Did we do something wrong in raising you?" It brought tears to my eyes because of course they didn't, they did an amazing job raising me! My thirst for existential knowledge is undeniable and I understand and appreciate how sometimes that can be misconstrued as a feeling of "wrong with". Throughout everything I've experienced and the total 180 shift of my being in the past 5 years and the highs and the lows, my parents have been there, maybe not always understanding why, but nonetheless always supportive!

Finally, I'd be remiss if I didn't acknowledge my clients. Thank you to my clients, both my 1:1 private coaching clients and my corporate clients. Seeing you all apply the teachings and experiencing positive shifts in your life keeps the fire burning deep within me!

Last but certainly not least, THANK YOU for taking the time to feel the message behind this book and to take these words to heart. It's within the integration (the taking action) that you will experience transformation. Thank you for showing up for yourself to honor your emotions and allow yourself the space and grace to process them to transmute them to transform your life into a deeper and more meaningful existence than you could have ever imagined.

ABOUT THE AUTHOR

At 31 years old, Sam made Silicon Valley's 40 under 40 list recognizing his serial entrepreneur drive and million dollar business, SwagWorx.com. Externally, Sam appeared successful. Internally, he was falling apart.

In 2019, a ruptured relationship revealed feelings of overwhelm that had been numbed by decades of indulgence in food, alcohol, and business achievements through workaholism. Ego aside, he embraced a path of self-discovery, spirituality, and soul purpose. An intentional journey that's culminated in a proven, minutes-long, 6-Step B.R.E.A.T.H. Process that now helps "busy professionals" access inner peace and "Overcome the Overwhelm," the title of his sixth book.

Passionate about bridging the gap between workplace culture and mental health, Sam's mission is to teach accessible tools that overcome overwhelm. His ultimate goal is to help eradicate the glorification of Hustle Culture while encouraging an expansion of Compassionate Leadership.

Sam is a certified yoga instructor, breathwork facilitator, podcaster, and keynote speaker. His book, "SOUL/Life Balance," is a No. 1 bestseller.

Learn more about his work at SamKabert.com.